WHAT TO DO WHEN I GET STUPID

A Radically Safe Approach
To a Difficult Financial Era

Lewis Mandell, Ph.D.

Point White

Publishing

Copyright © 2013 by Lewis Mandell

Published by Point White Publishing

All rights reserved. Printed in the United States of America. No part of this book may be reproduced, stored in a retrieval system or transmitted in any manner whatsoever without written permission except for brief quotations contained in reviews. For information, write to Point White Publishing, 3720 Point White Drive, Bainbridge Island, WA 98110.

Limit of Liability: While the author and publisher have prepared this book using their best efforts, they make no representations or warranties as to the completeness or accuracy of this book. Readers should note that any advice or strategies contained in this book may not be suitable for their situation. They should consult with professional advisors where appropriate.

Cover design from an original oil painting by Nancy A. Mandell

FIRST PAPERBACK EDITION

ISBN 978-0-9897427-2-6

Table of Contents

x

Acknowledgments

As I approached the final life cycle stage of retirement, I naturally began to think back to the retirement of my parents and marveled about how well they did without much retirement income. With little more than 40 or 50 percent of their pre-retirement income, largely from Social Security, they lived well and even managed to multiply their net worth in retirement. This seemed to fly in the face of much of the fear promoted by the financial services industry that retirement wasn't possible unless people could generate 75 percent or even more of what they earned in their last years of work. Something didn't jibe!

As I began working on a book to explain how people could enjoy a comfortable retirement with little more than Social Security income, a friend, identified here as "Phillip" asked me whether he should buy an annuity because he was afraid of "getting stupid" as he aged and doing dumb things with his money. It then occurred to me that age-related decrease in cognition was very much related to the entire retirement process which brought me to write this book.

A lot of people helped me think through this process and deserve thanks for their contributions. Waldo Klein, a gerontologist at the University of Connecticut, helped me understand the aging process and what to expect. I have profited from discussions from a variety of people on a variety of subjects. These include, in alphabetical order, Mary Collins Tom Forma, Richard Einziger Jim Kadlec, Malcolm McKinnon, Paul Merriman, Helaine Olen, Pamela Perun, Richard Peterson and Hersh Stern. Many of them have disagreed and will continue to disagree with some of my conclusions but I hope that they find parts of my analysis to be useful.

My friends Efrem Sigel and Michael Meyer read drafts of the book and made excellent stylistic suggestions. Finally, I owe a tremendous debt of gratitude to my wife, Nancy, who helped on every phase from encouragement to editing to the cover design that uses one of her oil paintings.

Introduction

Earlier this year my friend Philip, a 70-year old retired pediatrician, asked me whether I thought he should buy an annuity that would pay him a set amount of money every month for the rest of his life. "Philip," I replied, thinking in economist mode, "why in the world do you need an annuity, with all its fees, and why would you buy it now, with interest rates and annuity payments at an all-time low? You just took my investments course at the University of Washington and you should know better." Philip's sheepish response hit me like a two by four. "I want a dependable source of income *when I get stupid*."

However, Phillip got me thinking, and about a month or so later, my wife and I sat with our estate attorney making small changes in our wills. Out of the blue the attorney said "I see that you manage your own investments, which is great given your background, but what will happen in 5 or 10 years when you may not be up to it?" Note that she didn't add "when you get stupid," or "when age makes you more susceptible to high pressure sales techniques." She didn't have to because I had already started reading the literature, and it wasn't pretty.

1

Within the past couple of years, a number of prominent economists have begun to focus on our ability to make good financial decisions as we get older. This research is being done primarily by behavioral economists who increasingly find that we consumers do not always make financial decisions that are in our best interests. Some of our financial "mistakes" are due to our psychological makeup. We may buy too much on credit because we value the immediate gratification of a purchase far more than the delayed pain of repayment. Or we may get carried away by the rising prices of high tech stocks or real estate.

Some of our financial mistakes are due to the complexity of today's financial instruments such as mortgages and 401(k) retirement plans. Add to this the financial illiteracy that many individuals have. My own research over the past 18 years has focused on financial literacy and how difficult it is to teach even bright and well-educated people what they need to know to handle their own affairs. In fact, relatively few appear willing to put in the effort to learn.

However, until recently I was unaware of how rapidly age decreases our ability to make sound financial choices. Psychologists have long known that our cognitive or reasoning ability peaks at about age 20, which is why the great mathematical discoveries tend to be made by younger scholars. Fortunately for most of us, along with age comes experience which helps us make better decisions. When we put cognitive ability and experience together and focus on *financial* decisions, research indicates that we peak at about age 53 and decline thereafter at a pretty rapid rate. A minority of us can expect to reach age 80 without some type of mental impairment that will cloud our financial decision-making.

To make matters worse, as our ability to make sound financial decisions decreases with age, our self-confidence in this area actually increases. It is therefore wise of us to take future financial decision-making out of our own hands while we still have the mental capacity to do so. This doesn't mean moving immediately to a nursing home and giving all our wealth to our children, like Shakespeare's King Lear who lived to regret it when his daughters wouldn't take him in. Rather, it does mean that we should become aware of the options we have to guarantee an adequate, regular income for the rest of our lives. Ideally, we would like to do it at the most reasonable cost, particularly since average investment returns for most older investors, who are naturally risk-averse, have been relatively low for more than a decade and are likely to remain low for much of our futures. If a broker, investment manager or financial planner takes a large chunk of that return in the form of fees and commissions, this can greatly reduce the incomes left for us to live on, so we must carefully evaluate the costs and benefits of the services offered to us by money managers.

Our book will begin with a more complete discussion of when and how our financial ability is likely to decline. Anticipating this decline, we need to make some critical decisions *now* to guarantee that we will have enough income coming in each month, for the rest of our lives, to maintain our basic or "core" standard of living. The guaranteed income must be regular and dependable, must last for our lives *no matter how long we live*, must be virtually impossible to lose, either through a swindler or our own diminished judgment in the future, and, ideally, it must increase as our expenses increase with inflation. We will see how a fully-paid age-in-place home may be the single best investment we can make.

Finally, we will look at the costs and benefits of using professional advisors, including brokers, investment managers and financial planners. Though many of these professionals are good, they are often very expensive relative to the modest investment returns we can expect and may have interests that are not aligned with our own. If we still decide to use such advisors, we should be able to tell the advisors upfront what we want *them* to do for *us*, even if it is not in *their* best financial interests.

This book was written specifically for those retired or soon to be retired individuals (or their caring children) who have accumulated sufficient resources during their working years to be able to live safely, in reasonable comfort for the rest of their lives. It addresses, in very frank terms, a number of threats to our financial safety. One group of threats is our volatile and unpredictable economy with low interest rates, a volatile stock market, fluctuating tax policies and the possibility of a jump in inflation. Another important threat may result from our own good health and longevity which could cause us to outlive our sources of income. A final threat comes from those in whose hands we have entrusted our financial lives, including well-meaning or not so well-meaning brokers and financial advisors, or even ourselves as our mental facilities begin to deteriorate. By today's standards, this book is "radically safe" in its approach to handling all of these threats.

This is a short book that pulls no punches because the author is a well-known behavioral economist who is often credited with helping to found the new field of financial literacy. He really wrote the book for himself, to help *him* think through these complex but critical issues. The author has nothing to sell -- no financial products, no financial planning services and no tie-ins with organizations that sell financial products and services.

Chapter 1
When and How Does Financial Ability Decline?

At a Glance

As we move through middle age, our ability to manage our finances tends to peak, on average, shortly after our 53rd birthday and declines thereafter. By the time we hit 70, this rate of decline steepens precipitously.

The relationship between age and financial capability is a function of two offsetting aspects of intelligence. As we get older, experience makes us better able to cope with a variety of familiar problems. This is called "crystallized intelligence." However, past the age of 20, our analytical ability necessary to perform new tasks declines steadily. This is called "fluid intelligence." Since the intelligence we gain from experience increases more and more slowly after some three decades of adult experience, our steadily declining fluid intelligence ultimately offsets the gains from experience, causing most of the decline in our financial capability.

Hastening this decline is the beginning of age-related neurological problems including dementia and other types of cognitive impairment.   Overall cognitive impairment increases from 21 percent of those in our 70's, to 53 percent of those in our 80's and 76 percent of those over 90.

The ability to make investment decisions has been found to peak at about age 70, somewhat later than other types of financial decisions such as those that relate to the use of debt. This is probably due to the fact that many adults focus on their investments only later in life when they have both assets and the time to think about them. Unfortunately, studies have found that as people get older, their confidence in their abilities to make good investment and insurance choices actually *increases* as their measured ability decreases, leading to the likelihood of poor outcomes.

In part because of increased confusion as we age, we become more susceptible to sales pitches and pressure put on us by those who target older people with assets. Investment fraud has become epidemic in the US, victimizing more than 13 percent of the population each year. Investment fraud victims were found to be older, richer and better educated, demonstrating the Willie Sutton maxim that crooks always go to where the money is. Victims were also most likely to open themselves up to sales pressure by attending the free luncheons or dinners offered with sales seminars.

One in five Americans aged 65 or older has been taken advantage of financially in terms of an inappropriate investment, unreasonably high fees for financial services, or outright fraud. However, when asked whether they are worried that they will become less able to handle personal finances over time, nearly two-thirds of Americans of Medicare age answered "no."

This chapter tells us that no matter how smart, experienced or financially knowledgeable we are now, we are likely to be less so in the future. Therefore, we need to make some good, incorruptible plans for our future now, while we still have the ability to do so. And if we have a spouse, life partner or dependent who is less interested in or less knowledgeable about financial matters than we are, it is all the more important that we make decisions that will protect them as well.

Age-Related Decline in Financial Ability

As we get older, our ability to manage our finances is pulled in two opposite directions. On the positive side, experience that comes with age, often called "crystallized intelligence," helps us to recognize, anticipate and hopefully avoid problems we have encountered before. Some of this experience comes from repetition, such as negotiating an auto loan for a second time when we trade in our car. Some may come with mistakes that we, ourselves, have made, such as missing a credit card payment because we waited too long to mail it in. Additional experience may result from learning about the mistakes of others including celebrities taken to the cleaners by Bernie Madoff and his infamous Ponzi scheme.

Offsetting the benefits of experience-related crystallized intelligence are age-related declines in "fluid intelligence" which is the ability to think abstractly and deal with complex information around us. Fluid intelligence helps us perform tasks that are different from and often more complex than those that we confront on a daily basis, such as choosing a new kind of home mortgage or investing newly acquired money. Research has found that fluid intelligence peaks at about age 20 and declines by about 1 percentile per year thereafter.[1] This means that if a 20 year old is in the 90th percentile (top 10 percent) of the population in terms of fluid intelligence, he or she will fall, on average, to the 40th percentile by age 70, the 30th percentile by age 80 and the 10th percentile (lowest 10 percent in cognitive ability) by age 90. [2]

According to gerontologists (those who study older people), the aging process affects intelligence in two ways. General intelligence decreases with age as memory and attention weaken.[3]   In addition, our sensory abilities (vision and hearing) also deteriorate with age, contributing to a loss in our ability to observe and stay current. Declines in intelligence tend to become considerably steeper after age 70[4], although those who continue to pursue a profession, such as a doctor or a lawyer, can slow this decline in their area of strength through frequent practicing[5].

The cognitive decline of many older adults is hastened by age-related neurological problems including both "dementia," which refers to a serious decline in cognitive ability and less severe "cognitive impairment without dementia." Approximately 60 percent of dementia results from Alzheimer's disease while another 25 percent results from vascular (blood circulation) disease such as strokes. The incidence of dementia in the US population increases from 5 percent for those in their 70's to 29 percent of those in their 80's and 39 percent of those above age 90. [6]

If we add to those with dementia, people who suffer from cognitive impairment without dementia, we find that overall cognitive impairment increases from 21 percent of those in their 70's, to 53 percent of those in their 80's and 76 percent of those above 90.[7]

Overall Cognitive Ability

Our overall ability to deal with our finances depends on the relative impact of the two offsetting forces. Our fluid intelligence declines at a slow but steady pace from about age 20 while our crystallized intelligence increases with age and experience. It is not unreasonable to assume that most crystallized intelligence related to finances increases more rapidly in our early adult years than later in life. We begin to deal with a variety of financial problems such as mortgages, car loans, credit cards and 401(k) investments in our 20's and early 30's and learn a great deal from our "research" and early mistakes.

Since fluid intelligence declines at a slow but steady rate, overall intelligence will tend to increase at first, boosted by the relatively quick increase in crystallized intelligence, but then begins to slow down in middle age. The constant loss of fluid intelligence begins to match the smaller and smaller increases in crystallized intelligence until the increases and decreases are equal, at which point our overall intelligence peaks. Figure 1 shows that if we add these two types of intelligence together at each age, we should end up with an inverted "U" which peaks somewhere in middle age. We will see actual evidence below which estimates the average age at which our financial intelligence peaks.

Evidence on Age and Intelligence

The US Government's *Health and Retirement Study* (HRS) studies 22,000 Americans over age 50 every two years. Part of the study involves tasks that measure cognitive ability[8]. One such task involves "immediate word recall in

Figure 1
Hypothetical Illustration of Fluid Intelligence,
Crystallized Intelligence and Overall Intelligence
Related to Age

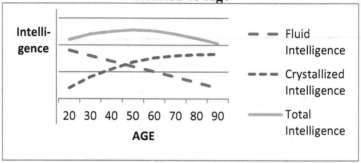

Source: Author

which the interviewer reads a list of 10 simple, unrelated nouns such as "lake, rope, and desk" and the respondent is immediately asked to recall as many from the list as possible. At age 51, the average person recalls 6.2 words out of 10. This drops to just 3 words out of 10 at age 90.

Age affects a 5-minute delayed word recall even more. Here, the average score fell from 5.4 out of 10 at age 51 to 2.1 of 10 at age 90. When asked to count backwards by 7 from 100, 51 year olds correctly calculated an average of 3.2 of the first 5 ("93, 86, 79, 72, 65") correctly, compared to 2.2 for the 90 year olds. In a test of practical arithmetic, people were asked "If the chance of getting a disease is 10 percent, how many people out of 1,000 would be expected to get the disease." Seventy nine percent answered correctly ("100") at age 63 compared to 50 percent at age 90. When asked how much money five winners of a $2 million lottery would each get if the money was split evenly, 52 percent gave the correct answer of

$400,000 at age 53, but by age 90, only 10 percent could answer this question correctly.

A subsample of the *Health and Retirement Study* respondents was given an in-person clinical assessment of cognitive function and dementia. The resultant Clinical Dementia Ratings were measured on a scale ranging from 0 (healthy) to 3, where 1 was mild, 2 moderate, and 3 severe dementia. At age 75 the average score was 0.4 which was just below the threshold for very mild dementia. This increased to 3.2 (severe dementia) at age 99.[9]

Financial Capability Peaks at 53

Using large data sets obtained from various financial institutions, a group of scholars[10] measured the age of peak performance of 10 credit-related financial tasks ranging from getting the best deals on home equity loans and lines, to knowing the best way to transfer credit card balances to a new card, to not paying late fees on credit cards. The age of peak performance varies by financial product decision from a low of 45.8 to a high of 61.8 years. The average peak performance age measured across all tasks was *53.3 years*.

Age and Investment Decisions

Thus far, we have seen evidence that our financial capability peaks at an average age of 53.3 for decisions related to the use of credit. Does age-related financial capability also decline in our later years for investment decisions? This is particularly important for many baby boomers and older Americans whose attention has turned from deciding how to borrow to deciding how to invest.

A well-known study of the actual investment decisions of older individual investors found that they had worse investment skills than younger investors[11]. They concluded that the adverse effects of aging tended to

11

outweigh the positive effects of experience. While older investors tended to begin with investment portfolios that reflected greater knowledge about investing, their subsequent investments showed decreasing levels of skill. This indicates that investment skills deteriorate with adverse effects of cognitive aging.

The study also found that older investors benefitted from their experience in a number of ways. In contrast to younger investors, they tended to hold less risky portfolios, traded less frequently and were more likely to do beneficial year-end tax loss selling. However, consistent with age-related loss of fluid intelligence, older investors had worse stock selection ability and poor diversification skills.

Overall investment skills tend to peak at around age 70. The fact that investment skills tend to peak some 16-17 years later than borrowing skills is probably due to the differing ages at which we gain experience in borrowing and investing. When we're young and don't have that much money, we're forced to learn how to borrow in order to finance many of the things that we need, including education, cars and homes. When we're older, at or near retirement, we don't need to borrow so much but finally have some assets accumulated for our retirement. It is at this age that many of us begin to pay attention to the financial news, attend legitimate financial seminars, and really begin to learn something about our investments. Therefore, our borrowing skills start to build early in life, in our 20's and early 30's, while our investment skills tend to build much later, often in our 50's and beyond.

Figure 2 gives an illustration of how investment intelligence may peak later than credit intelligence as the result of learning at an older starting age. While older investors are more likely than others to use beneficial investment "rules of thumb" that they've acquired through the years, they show less skill in implementing these rules, which is likely a sign of diminished fluid intelligence.

Figure 2
Hypothetical Illustration of Fluid Intelligence, Crystallized Credit and Investment Intelligence and Overall Credit and Investment Intelligence Related to Age

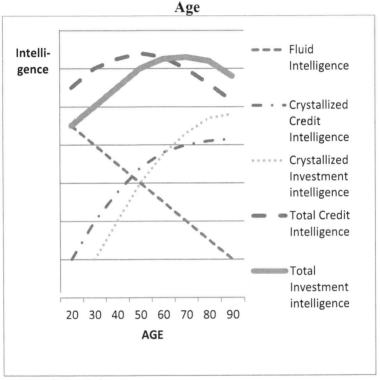

Source: Author

Older investors are more prone to attempt to use newer investment principals that they learn from TV, reading or seminars, such as the benefits of foreign investments. However, they are less skillful in using this information and may inadvertently end up adding to the overall riskiness of their investments.

Decline After 60

Financial literacy measures the ability of consumers to make financial decisions in their own best interests. As opposed to measuring actual behavior, financial literacy is based on answering a set of relevant and important questions correctly.

In 2012, Finke, Howe and Huston surveyed 6,335 respondents using the nationwide Consumer Finance Monthly Survey conducted by the Center for Human Resources Research at Ohio State University. They asked people of all ages a set of 20 financial questions relating to basics, investments, credit, and insurance. For example, when asked about the benefit of owning investments that are diversified, only a quarter said that it would reduce risk while the others incorrectly thought that diversification increased the rate of return or had tax benefits.[12]

The authors found a consistent annual decline in average financial literacy scores of about 1 percentage point per year among respondents over 60, regardless of level of education. This decline, if anticipated, need not necessarily lead to poor financial outcomes. "For example, recognition of diminished investment skills may increase demand for annuitization (converting financial assets into lifetime income) or the delegation of important financial decisions to a trusted advisor." [13] Unfortunately, *confidence* in financial decision-making abilities, particularly in the areas of investments and insurance, actually *increases* with age, as actual ability declines, leading to the likelihood of disastrous outcomes.

Getting older people to recognize the deterioration of their abilities is not easy. This can be seen among older drivers who do not generally perceive that their driving skills are deteriorating in spite of the decline in sensory ability that comes with more advanced age.[14] However, these same authors found that older drivers who took an objective test that demonstrated to them the decrease in their own driving skills tended to alter driving behavior to reduce the probability of their having an accident. This leads the authors to suggest that "It is possible that increased awareness of the natural decline in cognitive abilities essential to making effective financial decisions will lead to increased demand for more passive financial instruments such as annuities or passive investment vehicles that automatically rebalance."[15]

Undue Influence

Thus far we have seen that our cognitive ability, which determines how well we can handle our finances, tends to peak in middle age and decline rapidly past the age of 70. Why should this concern us?

I see two primary reasons for concern. First, and to my mind less importantly, as our financial skills slip, we will tend to become a little less prompt or reliable in tending to routine tasks. If one of our bonds matures, for example, we may take a while to replace it.

Of far greater importance is the fact that as we age, we become more susceptible to sales pitches and pressure put on us by those who target older people with assets. This benefits the scammers, crooks, psychopaths and sociopaths who specialize in elder fraud. In fact, a 2007 Federal Trade Commission study[16] found 13.3 percent of US population had fallen for a fraud scheme in the preceding 12 months. Surprisingly, a 2011 AARP study found that compared to the general population, investment fraud victims were older, richer, better educated and more likely to be male[17]. They were also most likely to open themselves up to sales pressure by attending the free luncheons or dinners offered with sales seminars.

A 2009 survey by AARP found that ten percent of Americans over the age of 55 had accepted a free investment seminar lunch or dinner in the past three years.[18] In her excellent book *Pound Foolish*, Helaine Olen explains that the purpose of these "free" seminars, generally held at good, well-known restaurants with easy-to-digest food, is to make the older Americans who accept the invitations feel guilty and want to give something back to the host in return.[19] If you are shopping for a financial advisor, why would you want to start off indebting yourself to an unknown salesperson in exchange for a $20 meal?

Somewhat more worrisome are the "legal fraudsters," the relatively small proportion of unscrupulous but licensed and credentialed brokers, financial planners, investment managers and insurance sellers who make money by getting you to do dumb things. Their sins can range from charging you a disproportionate share of your total returns for "managing" your money to "churning" your money into commissions through constant buying and selling, to selling you products with high commissions that you don't really want or need, to putting your money into deals that benefit them.

Finally, we will not be the first to tell you that lonely older people have been known to remarry and sign their remaining assets over to the new spouse, at the expense of their children and sometimes even themselves. A friend's father spent a successful career practicing law and prided himself on his knowledge and common sense. After he lost his wife in his late 70s, he began to decline slowly but convinced his children (and himself) that he was still a good custodian to himself and to the estate that he was preserving for them. At age 80 he met a well-educated, "classy" woman some 15 years younger than himself and shortly thereafter they were married.

She soon convinced him to make all of their assets marital property and within a year or so, his mental capacity had declined to the point where she was able to put him into a nursing home. The man's children ended up without a penny of the considerable estate their father had built and preserved for them.

When we think of all the ways we can hurt ourselves or our loved ones when we get "stupid," we should double our resolve to do something about it while we still have the cognitive capacity to do so.

Elder Fraud and Exploitation

A recent study by the Investor Protection Trust[20] found 20 percent of Americans aged 65 or older have "been taken advantage of financially in terms of an inappropriate investment, unreasonably high fees for financial services, or outright fraud." The susceptibility of older Americans to fraud is huge, with 57 percent of those over age 65 foolishly believing that "A very high rate of return is okay as long as the investment is guaranteed or bonded" even though the investment could be "guaranteed" or "bonded" by anyone.

Nearly half (46 percent) incorrectly think that "If an investment is registered with the SEC or state securities regulators, it been reviewed to make sure it's safe." "Legal" and "safe" are two different things as many people who have bought (legal) penny stocks have learned. A company that follows a set of legal requirements can be approved by the SEC to sell its shares to the public, even though its business is very risky.

In addition, 32 percent of seniors believed that "Variable annuities are usually good investments, especially for retirees." In fact, most variable annuities, which offer tax benefits to younger, working people who are accumulating retirement assets, are a terrible investment for retirees since they tend to be both risky and expensive and offer few tax benefits to those who no longer work.

When asked whether they are worried if they will become less able to handle personal finances over time, nearly two-thirds (63 percent) said "no." Clearly they have not yet read this chapter!

Conclusion

Sooner or later, probably past the age of 70, those of us who make our own financial decisions will find that our ability to do so is weakening. With luck, this will come on gradually and will be so apparent to us that we will take measures to protect ourselves against our own actions, very much as we instinctively hold tighter to handrails as we go down a steep flight of stairs or drive a little more slowly in the dark. Unfortunately, while the average cognitive or intellectual ability of the entire population appears to decline smoothly with age, each of us is unique and may suffer a sudden steep decline as the result of illness, depression or loss of reliable companions. We may also fall under the influence of someone who wants to own our assets.

Therefore, it is important to do certain things to protect ourselves now, while we still have the mental capacity to do so. In this book, we will see that the single most important thing we can do is to set up a *guaranteed* source of lifetime income for ourselves and our loved ones, no matter how long we live. It doesn't mean that we have to turn our assets over to a custodian which may, in itself, be fraught with peril.

Most of us will be able to handle our day-to-day finances for much of our remaining lives, paying bills, going on vacations and enjoying life. What we should avoid doing is leaving our core investments, needed to finance our basic standard of living, subject to our own unpredictable future whims or, worse, the future whims of someone else.

What to Do When I Get Stupid

Chapter 2
Rethinking Our Retirement

At a Glance

Since this book is about safety, it presents a retirement strategy that is somewhat safer and more targeted than the "balanced" portfolios currently promoted by most of the financial services industry. This is based on the author's observation that most people want, at minimum, a stream of income, guaranteed for life, which will enable them to continue living in comfort no matter how long they live. This guaranteed lifetime income is, in most ways, identical to Social Security retirement income and similar to many (traditional) defined benefit pensions which pay workers a fixed or increasing amount for the rest of their lives

The cost of "living in comfort" is the basis of our *core* annual retirement expenses. These include both what we spend on necessities as well as the traditional extras such as newspapers, cable or satellite TV, internet, basic transportation and occasional trips to see the kids, that we feel are essential to maintaining what we consider to be a minimally-acceptable standard of living.

Our fundamental, unalterable objective is to have at least enough money coming in every year of our lives to guarantee coverage of (at least) our core retirement expenses. We want to take no chances with this critical stream of income, *none whatsoever.* Beyond that, any additional retirement income becomes discretionary and can be used to increase our standard of living or, if sufficient, even fulfill whatever dreams we might have. These "dreams" might include trips and toys and vacation homes, or an estate for our heirs, charitable bequests or even an attempt to beat the market and become seriously rich.

In this book we put the discretionary assets that are *above* those needed to fund our core retirement expenses into a separate "bucket" that we do not mingle with our core assets. With these *surplus* assets we can take whatever risk we want, realizing that risk and reward tend to be correlated over time. However, we try not to risk even a penny of the assets needed to fund our core retirement expenses. Risk and reward may be correlated over time, but the period of time in which taking greater risk results in greater returns may be extremely long, far exceeding the remaining lives of retirees. Therefore, we go against the prevailing wisdom offered by companies that sell stocks and mutual funds to maintain a *balance* of both stocks and bonds that is based on the risk we are willing to take. Unless we have enough guaranteed, lifetime income to cover our core retirement expenses, I feel that we have no business holding even 1 percent of our assets in the form of stocks. Hopefully, I will convince you of the wisdom of this approach and show you ways in which you can use your limited assets to achieve a totally secure retirement, no matter how long you live.

We live in volatile, economically dangerous times and don't know when, if ever, these times will end. Stocks, which returned nearly 11 percent per year from 1926 to 1999, barely returned 5 percent in the next dozen years and fell in value by half in 2008. Bank savings accounts pay virtually zero and even 10 year Treasury Bonds have recently been paying little more than 2 percent. The Federal Reserve finds it difficult to reduce our high rates of unemployment, even with a huge expansion of the money supply, and the Federal government's fiscal policy is handcuffed by a politically-divided Congress and sky-high national debt. This is not the time to be *betting* the assets we need on risky investments – not even half of our assets in a so-called "balanced" portfolio.[21]

If we don't have enough guaranteed income to cover our core expenses for the rest of our lives, we can convert some of our assets, which may now be at some risk, into guaranteed lifetime income to try to close this gap. The most efficient way to do this is through the purchase of immediate fixed annuities which will be explained later in this chapter. If we still lack sufficient income to cover our core lifetime expenses, we must find the least unpleasant ways to cut back. For most of us, this involves downsizing to a fully-paid off home in which we can *age in place*. In many instances, a home of this type also enables us to avoid or minimize long-term care insurance which is becoming increasingly expensive. More on this later.

While inflation has not been much of a problem in the US since the mid-1980s, it may well come back again, hurting the standard of living of retirees with fixed incomes. Since the economic collapse of 2008, the Federal Reserve has greatly increased the money supply through "Quantitative Easing." We have been through at least three phases of quantitative easing known as "QE1," "QE2" and "QE3" during which time the "Fed" has pumped huge amounts of money into the economy in an attempt to keep interest rates down to stimulate investment in business, housing and consumption. In the US, this rapid increase in the money supply has not yet resulted in inflation since high levels of unemployment and reduced consumer demand keep wages and prices low. However, when the US economy recovers, many economists expect to see inflation increase to an annual rate of 3 or 4 percent or more. At just 4 percent inflation, prices will double in 18 years.

Some types of lifetime income offer protection from inflation by adjusting automatically to increases in the cost of living. These include Social Security retirement income, defined benefit pension income with cost of living adjustments (COLAs), and fixed annuity income which adjusts for inflation. *Probably the best way to protect against inflation is to minimize core expenses by owning much of what we need outright,* including a low-maintenance, low energy home, durable furniture and a long-lasting car. This inflation-protection can be supplemented through the ownership of US Treasury Inflation Protected Securities (TIPS) whose principal and interest adjust automatically to inflation.

Funding Core Expenses

If Chapter 1 has you concerned about doing something so stupid that it can screw up your retirement, it means that you have some sort of retirement strategy in mind, even if it isn't a formal, written plan. For most of us, the basic strategy is to have enough money coming in to maintain a comfortable standard of living for the rest of our lives.

This chapter is important to you because you want enough *guaranteed* money coming in each year to live in comfort and because you want to live in comfort for the rest of your life, *no matter how long you live.*

Living in Comfort

What does it mean to live in comfort? On one hand, this can be seen as a highly subjective question that will differ for every person, depending on the standard of living they have enjoyed to this point and their retirement aspirations. Some of us have fantasies of an idyllic retirement on a tropical beach, a deluxe apartment in the Manhattan sky, a permanent condo on an ocean-going cruise ship or a house next door to our children and grandchildren. Others of us have a bucket list of things we want to accomplish while we still can, such as visiting the Holy Land or Antarctica, learning to fly or mastering a foreign language.

Unfortunately, most of us are limited by finite resources – our income and the assets we have that can generate income. Therefore, we will start by estimating what it takes (or will take for those who are not yet retired) to "live in comfort." Since this term is necessarily vague, we will begin by using our current expenses minus any "frills" that we could do without, if necessary, without significantly compromising our ability to live in comfort. "Frills" might include vacations, eating out in expensive restaurants, multiple cars, etc., but, again, this is highly subjective. If you have not yet retired, assume that you will

25

remain in your current home unless you have made definite plans to move.

The current cost of living in no-frills comfort is what we will define as our *core* annual retirement expenses. Our fundamental objective is to have enough money coming in every year of our lives to guarantee coverage of these core retirement expenses. In this way we can be sure to live in reasonable comfort for the rest of our lives, no matter how long we live. Hopefully we will find that we have enough regular income to do *more* than cover our core expenses so that we can afford our current extra expenses and don't have to economize in any way on the standard of living that we currently enjoy. If we have more than enough income to support our current standard of living, we can do additional things like going on long or exotic vacations, buying a larger home or a second home, giving money to the kids or trying to get rich (or richer).

However, if we cannot generate enough guaranteed lifetime income to cover our core expenses, we have but two choices: (1) we can reduce our standard of living to a sustainable, but less desirable level, with a smaller home (including an apartment type of home such as a condominium or cooperative), a single car (or no car at all), and few, if any restaurant meals, or (2) we can *gamble* on our futures by investing in *risky* assets, such as stocks, that may or may not pay off but which will not give us a *guaranteed* return for life. It is interesting to note that most Americans who retire with financial assets choose number (2), the gamble. This may be due to the fact that relatively few are aware of or willing to choose the safer option.

Some knowledgeable but risk-loving retirees may be willing to roll the dice to possibly increase (or decrease) their standard of living in retirement. As we will see in Chapter 4, many of those who give financial advice to retirees, including stockbrokers, financial planners and investment advisors, make their living by selling and managing risky assets. Their advice may even encourage a client's propensity toward betting the future on risky investment returns.

Estimating Core Retirement Expenses

If you are like me, and own your home outright, without a mortgage, you'll be amazed to learn just how low your core expenses are (or will be) in retirement. This is very good news for many retirees and is completely at variance with those who push stocks and other risky assets to retirees, repeating the gamble-inducing myth that we need at least our pre-retirement income to survive our golden years. In fact, my wife's and my Social Security alone nearly covers our personal core expenses, as it did for my parents and does for most of my friends. I bet you don't read this very often!

It is important to have an estimate of our core expenses since this is the amount of money that we must have for the rest of our lives to maintain our accustomed lifestyle. We will begin by estimating how many thousand dollars we now spend on each category, if we are retired, or plan to spend when we do retire. Chart 1 gives a picture of what our annual core expenses might look like.

Table 1, below, first divides our expenses into broad categories, such as housing, transportation, food, etc. and then divides them into specific items such as mortgage payments, real estate taxes and insurance for the home. Your job is to come up with a rough estimate how many thousands of dollars they cost (or will cost when you retire). Look up the numbers later, if you want, but a quick and dirty estimate is all that you need now. Although I'm

Chart 1
Estimated Annual Core Expenses

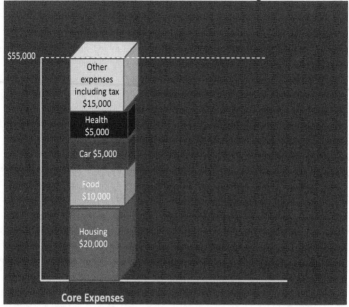

certain that my readers don't really need my help, I have provided a little guide with Table 1 that can help jog your memory about your annual expenses.

Add together your core expenses (third column) and you will have an estimate of the annual income you will need for every year of your retirement.

Inflation and Retirement Expenses

Put a check mark in the final column ("Inflatable") if the core expenses will increase with inflation. This should apply to almost all the items with the possible exception of mortgage or other fixed (not adjustable) loan payments, if you have them.

Historically inflation, particularly sudden, unanticipated inflation, has hit retired persons living on

Table 1
Annual Retirement Expenses

Item	Core Annual Expenses ($1,000s)	Inflatable? (check)
Rent		√
Mortgage		
Property Taxes[a]		√
Home Insurance[a]		√
Home Utilities[b]		√
Home Maintenance[c]		√
Home - Other[d]		√
Groceries[e]		√
Restaurant		√
Car payment		√
Car Insurance[f]		√
Gas & Oil		√
Car Maintenance		√
Clothing[g]		√
Health Insurance		√
Medical/Dental[h]		√
Medications		√
Income Tax		√
Other[i]		√
TOTAL		

[a]Unless included in mortgage payment [b]Include heating, gas and electricity [c] Include yard-work and HOA fees (less taxes) [d]Include household and yard help [e]Include alcoholic beverages [f]Unless included in car payment [g]For all family members [h]Include co-pays and non-reimbursed payments. [i]Include travel and anything else not mentioned above. Don't include income taxes a second time.

29

What to Do When I Get Stupid

Social Security fixed incomes the hardest. While the rate of inflation has not been great for the last 30 years, it did reach 13.58 percent in 1980. At this high rate, the purchasing power of a fixed pension will be cut in half in about 5 1/3 years.

To protect older Americans from inflation, Social Security payments are indexed to the cost of living. This means that if inflation goes up by 5 percent in a year, retirement payments will go up by 5 percent, starting the following year. And since Medicare provides most medical payments for Americans over age 65, another large category of expense has been removed from the ravages of inflation.

Social Security and Inflation

Social Security retirement benefits are currently adjusted for inflation according to changes in the Consumer Price Index for urban wage and clerical workers, abbreviated as "C.P.I.-W." This is calculated by the Bureau of Labor Statistics based on two surveys. The first survey asks workers (but not retirees) what they buy and these results are used to put together an average "market basket" of goods typically purchased by urban workers. The second survey is of prices in urban supermarkets and other places where urban workers buy the goods in their market basket. By measuring the prices of goods in the average market basket monthly, the federal government comes up with the urban Consumer Price Index. This index was set at 100 based on average prices in the 1982-1984 period. In 2012 it was 224.6 which means that prices more than doubled since 1982-84.

Many economists have pointed out that consumers change what they buy in response to changes in the prices of the goods in their market basket. For example, if a family buys steak once a week and the price of steak goes

30

up while the price of chicken stays the same, the family would tend to buy less steak and more chicken because chicken has become a better value. Therefore, economists claim, the CPI *overstates* inflation since it assumes that consumers still buy as much steak, whose price has gone up, while they are actually saving money by buying less steak and more chicken, whose price has stayed the same.

Since Social Security is expected to have some financial difficulties in the future, those seeking to keep it solvent, including President Obama, have proposed to change the Consumer Price Index to which it is linked. By switching to a slightly different (and more accurate) measure of inflation -- known as the "chained C.P.I.-U" -- Social Security's actuaries estimate it could reduce the program's current shortfall by about 20 percent by adjusting benefits to the cost of the average market basket *after* accounting for substitutions that consumers have actually made in their purchases based upon the relative changes of the prices of goods that they buy.

Although the proposed C.P.I. – U will include retirees (who are excluded from the C.P.I.-W index currently in use), there are two major problems for retirees with the switch to a chained price index. Since those who are retired tend to have different market baskets from working people (they spend more on health care and less on commuting, for example), the existing index, which is heavily weighted toward workers, will continue to understate the rapid inflation in health care. Second, if the cost of health care makes up a large part of the overall expenditures of retirees and that cost increases more rapidly than other goods (as it has in recent years), there are few ways the retiree can save money by substituting other, cheaper goods. If the cost of medications goes up faster than the cost of chicken, you can't buy more chicken and fewer pills!

Bottom line – a switch to the chained CPI will be costly for most retirees, if it occurs. According to calculations by Social Security analysts, workers retiring at age 65 would, after 10 years, receive 3.7 percent less in benefits than under the current (unchained) system. After 20 years, this difference would be 6.5 percent and after 30 years, it would be 9.2 percent less.[22] The strong possibility that this switch will be made to help prop up the finances of the Social Security System makes it even more important for retirees and those who will soon retire to take actions to protect themselves against inflation.

Pensions

Pensions vary in their ability to protect retirees against inflation. Many of today's retirees (but very few of tomorrow's) are still receiving a *defined benefit pension* which pays them a certain amount of money per month for life. Since defined benefit pensions are generally based on both final salary and number of years worked, they do tend to provide some protection against inflation *while the employee is still working* since salaries tend to go up with the cost of living and benefits are based on final salaries. However, after retirement, the purchasing power of a defined benefit pension which makes fixed payments will decrease with inflation.

A few pensions have defined benefits which are adjusted for inflation. This adjustment is called a "Cost of Living Adjustment" or COLA. COLA's are not commonly found in private sector pension plans. This forces recipients of defined benefit plans which are not adjusted for inflation to depend more on Social Security and private investments to keep retirement income equal to the cost of living.[23]

These days, most workers with pensions have *defined contribution* pensions which provide *no* guaranteed income for life. Rather, workers pay into a plan at work, most usually a 401(k) plan, and these retirement savings, which may be partly or fully matched by the employer, are invested for the worker's retirement. At retirement, the worker can take all or part of the accumulated funds and purchase an annuity which will provide income for life. And, as we will see later in this book, the worker can even purchase an annuity with a cost of living adjustment, just like the COLA of a defined benefit pension. However, unlike a defined benefit pension, whose monthly income is based on final salary and number of years worked, the income from an annuity purchased from the proceeds of a defined contribution plan depends on how much the employee contributed, how much of that contribution the employer matched, and how well the employee's investments have done. And, as we will also see, *very few workers with defined contribution pension plans purchase an annuity,* which means that few have regular, dependable lifetime retirement income from their pensions. An even smaller proportion (well under 1 percent) of workers with defined contribution pensions purchase annuities with cost of living adjustments, which means that most have significant inflation exposure.

Inflatable Expenses

Most retirement expenses go up with inflation. In this book we call expenses that go up with inflation "inflatables." To cover our inflatable core expenses for the rest of our lives, we need inflatable income, such as Social Security, pensions with COLAs or income from Treasury Inflation Protected bonds known as "TIPS" which increase both the interest they pay and their value as the cost of living goes up.

However, some of our retirement expenses, such as fixed rate mortgages and car loans, are not inflatable. These are easier to pay for with income that isn't inflatable.

Inflation-Protecting Core Income

Insurance is what we generally buy to protect ourselves against possible, but low probability losses such as our house burning down or our car being stolen. However, there are certain calamities for which regular insurance is not generally available. Inflation is one of these. Therefore, to protect ourselves against unanticipated inflation, we must take actions in advance that will counter its effects. These actions are known as "hedges."

Hedging strategies designed to deal with inflation in retirement depend upon the extent to which retirement expenses vary with inflation. If, for example, a retired couple has a fixed rate mortgage, their basic mortgage payment cannot go up with inflation. Therefore, fixed income in the form of defined benefit pension payments, fixed annuities, or even long-term bonds can be used to make those payments without risk of inflation.

For most retirees, the bulk of their expenses are subject to inflation since they include items such as real estate taxes, insurance, food, clothing, rent, travel, gasoline, household help, health care and so on. If these inflatable expenses are more than matched by Social Security retirement income, they are hedged against inflation since Social Security adjusts automatically to offset inflation. Therefore, our primary concern is with inflatable expenses that are *not* covered by inflation-protected income.

Retire Debt and Rent Free

In this chapter we show the importance of having low core expenses in retirement if we want to maintain our basic standard of living for the rest of our lives. An important way to achieve this is to be debt free, rent-free and lease-free. Why is this so?

Simply stated, if we own outright every physical thing that we need (home, car, furniture, appliances, clothing, etc.), we not only reduce our total expenses tremendously, *we also reduce our exposure to inflation.* This simple realization cannot be overemphasized, and it is one of a handful of critical retirement survival techniques.

In the United States, paying as much as 40 percent of your income for housing is considered to be normal. Many of us did this when we were young with growing families and growing incomes. Think of how much better we could have done if we had been able to own our home, outright, through our adult lives. In many cases, by not making mortgage payments, our housing-related expenses could have been cut by 75 percent or more.

To reiterate, because you haven't heard this very often, our standard of living in retirement is *not based on what we make or what we spend.* Rather, it is based on what we spend *and* the benefits we get from the things that we own outright such as housing. Economists call the income that we get from owning our home outright and not having to pay rent on it "implicit income." Since we already own so much of what we use in retirement (home, car, furniture, appliances, clothes), the money income that we will need to support ourselves in comfort in retirement may be far, far less than the income we made while we were working and paying for all of these things. So much for those fear-mongers who insist that we must have cash retirement income equal to 70 or so percent of our pre-retirement income!

A Home to Age in Place

For a lot of reasons, those who are retired or about to retire should look to buy a home with the following characteristics:

- It can be paid for in cash
- It is low maintenance and energy efficient
- It is suitable for aging in place

We have already covered some of the advantages of owning a home outright in retirement. For one thing, it really reduces our need for income since we no longer have to pay the mortgage. Also, it protects us against inflation since we don't have to worry about the landlord raising our rent.

The benefits of low maintenance speak not only to reduced core retirement expenses but also look to the future when those of us who can cut the grass, clean the gutters and fix the plumbing ourselves in early retirement will have to pay to have it done in a decade or so. The benefits of energy efficiency include a reduction in current core expenses and, equally important, a hedge against possible increases in energy costs in the future.

As the American population ages, it will become increasingly difficult to hire unskilled or semi-skilled workers to do housework, yard work and home maintenance. Furthermore, the cost of hiring this type of help will probably increase more rapidly than overall inflation. This means that an investment in a low-maintenance home (little landscaping, few repairs) will save us a lot of money in the future, particularly as the cost of help is likely to skyrocket.

"Aging in place" refers to our ability to live safely and comfortably in our homes as we get older, often to the very end of our lives. Homes that are suitable for aging in place are those that are "accessible" to us as our mobility decreases. Accessible homes include those on a single story which remove the dangers and effort of climbing stairs on creaky legs. Multi-level homes with a master bedroom on the first floor as well as homes with elevators are also suitable for aging in place, but tend to be more costly than single story homes. Other features of accessible houses include the absence of stairs to get in or out, good lighting, wide doorways for walkers and wheelchairs and walk-in showers or baths.

Many apartment-style homes are well-suited to aging in place. This is particularly true if they have elevators, an absence of stairs, wide doorways, professional maintenance and a gardening crew. Some condominium complexes in areas that are attractive to retirees, such as Florida, Arizona and California, cater specifically to retirees who are looking for affordable homes in which they can age in place. Many have security forces to protect residents as well as transportation to grocery stores, restaurants and health services. Some have health clinics on site along with emergency buzzers that can summon help, if needed. Most have other shared amenities such as clubhouses, swimming pools, tennis courts and perhaps even golf courses. Ownership costs can be surprisingly low compared to owning a house since they require tiny amounts of real estate, have far less square footage, share walls and energy costs along with maintenance costs and amenities. My folks lived in a 2 bedroom, 2 bath age-in-place condominium on the golf course of an attractive, gated community in south Florida. Their unit was just re-

bout $50,000 showing that aging in place in
ed not be prohibitively expensive.

ning an accessible home in which we can age in
place is important to keeping our future core expenses
down. In many cases, with an accessible home, we can
keep our loved ones or ourselves out of expensive nursing
homes which can quickly deplete needed assets. There are
many excellent books on the architecture and design of
aging in place that can give us advice.

Guaranteed Income for Core Expenses

Retired people should not have to gamble with the
income needed to fund their core expenses! *Not even a
little!*

This is the reasoning behind Social Security which
gives us a guaranteed income, adjusted for inflation, for the
rest of our lives, no matter how long we live. It is our
dependable safety net that no one can diminish or take
away from us, no matter how stupid we become. If a
financial advisor of any type asks you how much risk you
are willing to take with assets used to fund your core
retirement expenses, tell that advisor "none" and go find
another advisor. This is not the way the game is played!

Unless we are still paying on loans in retirement (a
bad idea), virtually all of our core expenses will be
inflatable, so the *core income* we will need to fund these
expenses for life should also be inflatable and must last for
life. Therefore, the ideal source of core income is a
lifetime *annuity* which guarantees the same income every
year for life, *adjusted for the cost of living*. Social Security
retirement income is just such an annuity as is a defined
benefit pension with a cost of living adjustment.[24]

38

Are You Set for Life?

Here comes the big test, your final exam, as it were. Do you have enough core income to cover your core retirement expenses for the rest of your life?

To keep things simple, let's not worry about inflation at this point. We will compare our annual core retirement expenses with our annual core retirement income from sources such as Social Security, defined benefit pensions, fixed annuities and income from reliable sources such as federal, high investment grade municipal and corporate bond interest, dividends from well-established companies and rental income. If core income is equal to or greater than core expenses, we are in good shape. If core expenses are higher, we have a deficit that must be overcome. In the Chart 2 example, below, core expenses are $55,000 per year and core income is only $45,000 per year leaving a deficit of $10,000.

There are a number of ways to make up the deficit. If you have financial assets invested in stocks, bonds, CDs or mutual funds, you may want to use them to purchase a single-payment immediate fixed annuity (*not a variable annuity*) which can significantly increase your lifetime, secure income. If you are currently receiving a return on your financial investments of 4 percent, and this just isn't enough to cover your core expenses, you really may be able to convert these assets into an annuity that can give you a guaranteed payment of nearly *twice as much* (depending on your age) for the rest of your life! This neat trick will be covered in the next chapter. Some people have decided to work a few extra years, if possible, to accumulate assets to close the deficit. Others have decided to downsize the home to reduce the size of their largest retirement expense.

Chart 2
Core Income, Expenses and Deficit

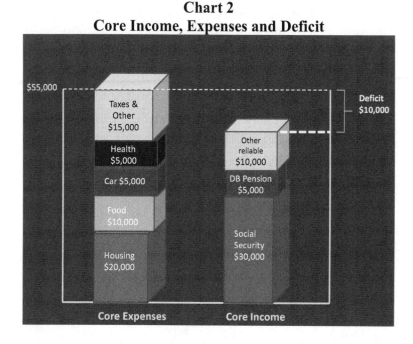

Dealing with the Inflation Problem

Our major retirement objective is to fund core retirement expenses with core retirement income. If we have a deficit, our primary objective is to find additional sources of reliable lifetime income or, if necessary, cut back on some of our expenses.

Once we have eliminated our *overall* retirement deficit, we can deal with a secondary, but still important problem, which is to make sure that our retirement income can fully fund our retirement expenses *in the event of inflation.*

In Table 1, we listed our core retirement expenses and determined which of those were "inflatable" or went up with inflation. We decided that most, if not all of these expenses were inflatable, the only exceptions being payments that we must make in fixed amounts such as mortgage or auto loan payments. Chart 3, below, gives us an example of a total of $55,000 in core retirement expenses of which $45,000 is inflatable and $10,000 is fixed.

If our inflatable core income matched our inflatable core expenses *and* our fixed core income matched our fixed core expenses, we would be in great shape, but this doesn't often happen. Even better, if our core inflatable income met all of our core retirement needs, inflatable and fixed, we would be in fat city since inflation couldn't hurt us. However, if our core inflatable expenses exceeded our core inflatable income, we do have some inflation exposure to deal with. In the example given in Chart 3, we have a $5,000 inflatable deficit and a $5,000 fixed deficit. If we have the assets, we might consider closing the fixed deficit by purchasing a *fixed* annuity that paid $5,000 per year for life and closing the $5,000 inflatable deficit with an annuity that paid $5,000 per year, adjusted for inflation.

What happens, however, when we have enough core retirement income to cover all of our expenses, but some of our retirement income is fixed while much or all of our retirement expenses are inflatable? This is a common problem for those who have some Social Security income, which is inflatable, but whose remaining income is fixed, as in the case of defined benefit pension payments which lack a COLA. This is also a difficult problem with few solutions offered in today's marketplace. One possible but inexact solution is to convert fixed income to inflatable income by investing in TIPS – Treasury bonds whose payment and principal automatically adjust to inflation. This will be covered in some detail in Chapter 5.

41

Chart 3
A Deficit in both Fixed and Inflatable Income

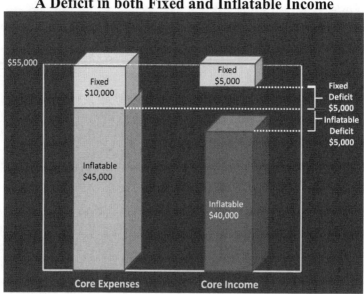

As we will see, the cost of "inflation insurance" is high, no matter how you choose to pay for it. A far better way to reduce our need for inflation protection is to reduce our core expenses that are subject to inflation, particularly if our core inflatable income is below our core inflatable expenses. This can be done, as indicated earlier, by owning a paid-up, low-maintenance, age-in-place home and ideally by living near mass transit.

A third realization, which will become clearer in the next chapter, is that it is possible, but more expensive, to buy a lifetime stream of income that is protected against inflation. Another option, covered in Chapter 5, shows how the purchase of TIPS (Treasury Inflation protected Securities) can compensate for the fact that some of our retirement income is fixed and will not adjust to cover inflation.

Hedging Fixed Retirement Expenses

While inflatable retirement expenses may be offset by Social Security payments and pensions with COLAs, fixed retirement expenses (such as a fixed-rate mortgage) are more easily offset by regular defined benefit pensions or the income on very secure bonds such as regular (non-TIPS) Treasury bonds. However, if a person has the assets to pay off a fixed debt, such as a mortgage, it is important to ask why they don't. Some will tell you that today's mortgage rates are so low (often under 4 percent), that they prefer to use the cheap money to invest in stocks. However, this is equivalent to borrowing money to play the slots. You may win, but if you lose, you will lose big! Just remember that stocks fell by half when the financial crisis hit in 2008. Yes, they finally came back in 2013 but they could easily decline again. In this book we *never* recommend gambling with income needed to cover our core retirement expenses, which means we should pay off all debts if we have the assets to do it.

There will be very few exceptions to this rule. If you own bonds that pay more than the cost of your mortgage, it means that the bonds are probably not totally safe[25]. In very recent times we have seen the bonds of some of the biggest, most stable companies in our country, such as Enron and Lehman Brothers, become virtually worthless. The municipal bonds issued by some of our largest cities have also defaulted. The only absolutely safe bond is a Treasury bond and if you own enough Treasuries to pay off your debts, why don't you?

Some people hate to give up their home mortgages because interest is tax deductible. However, this reasoning is faulty. If someone has a mortgage of $200,000 and also has $200,000 in cash, that person could pay off the mortgage with the cash, or invest the cash and keep the tax deduction on the mortgage. However, since the income from the assets in which they have invested their cash is taxable, the tax savings becomes a wash. Some more sophisticated homeowners might invest the money they borrowed through their home mortgage in tax-exempt municipal bonds which now pay rates as high as comparable Treasury bonds. However, there is a reason why some tax-exempt municipal bonds pay rates as high as Treasury bonds, and that is because they have become less and less safe as municipalities start to default as the result of huge pension and other obligations. Think Detroit! Again, how much risk do you want to take with your core standard of living in retirement? Think twice before taking out a mortgage, even a low-rate mortgage, if you have the ability to buy your home outright and carry no debt.

And remember from our discussion above, the major risks of carrying a home mortgage when you have the cash to pay it off but, instead, invest the cash, is not only the risk of losing money you have invested, it is also the risk that home values will fall again in another economic crisis. If you are leveraged, your home equity could rapidly fall to zero or even become negative, risking your other assets as well in many states. Only ten states have non-recourse laws which prevent a lender from coming after your other assets, or claiming part of your salary, if you walk away from your mortgage. These states include Alaska, Arizona, California, Hawaii, Minnesota, Montana, North Dakota, Oklahoma, Oregon, and Washington. In all other states, if you don't pay off your mortgage, you can lose just about everything else you own *in addition to your house.*

44

Long-Term Care Insurance

If we have carefully funded our core retirement expenses with a combination of Social Security retirement benefits, pensions, TIPS and annuities, and have no debt, we should be in pretty good shape. About the only risk to a secure retirement is the possibility that we or our partner may require expensive nursing care treatment for a long period of time. At an annual cost that can approach or exceed $100,000 per year for care in an Alzheimer unit, our carefully-constructed plans can be shot to hell.

Long-Term Care Insurance has become very expensive as the result of increased longevity. According to the American Association of Retired persons (AARP), the average annual cost for long-term care insurance that pays a maximum of only $150/day for up to 3 years[26] *and won't pay for the first 90 days*, is summarized in Table 2, below:

Table 2
Long-Term Care Premiums

Age of Purchase	Annual Premium
60	$1936
65	$2761
70	$4411
75	$7291

Source: AARP Guide to Long-Term Care
http://www.guidetolongtermcare.com/aarp.html.
Rates for couples may be up to 30 percent per person less than for individuals

Remember, the total amount that such a policy will pay you if you remain in a nursing home for the 3 full years (after your first 90 uncompensated days) is just $164,250

($150/day times 365 days in a year times 3 years). Therefore, if you have that in liquid assets per person (not needed to fund core expenses), you can self-insure for that 3-year period[27].

According to Prescott Cole in a recent article in the Wall Street Journal, the probability of collecting on such a long-term care policy is low since "...67 percent to 70 percent of seniors who do go into a nursing home are discharged within 90 days (i.e., before the policy begins to pay), and that after two years, less than 6 percent of those admitted will still be there. Actually, out of 40 million American seniors alive today, approximately 1.5 million currently live in nursing homes, about 3.7 percent."[28]

If your objective is to completely cover your core retirement expenses, you will probably need more coverage than $150/day (even adjusted for inflation) and will *definitely* need more than 3 years of total coverage to cover the unlikely, but extremely expensive possibility that nursing home care will be needed for many years. For a single person, moving to a nursing home for care of indefinite length (as in the case of Alzheimer's) generally means that the former residence can be sold, and nearly all needs will be provided by the nursing home or paid for by Medicare. Lifetime income can now be used to offset the cost of the nursing home. Once your assets are exhausted, you are generally moved onto Medicaid, so the only need to protect assets is to leave an inheritance. Therefore it may not be financially beneficial for a single person to pay for long-term care insurance.[29]

Long-term care insurance may be of greater importance in protecting the ability of a spouse or partner of the afflicted person to fund core expenses for life. If one partner goes into a nursing home for several years, it can easily drain the family's resources, leaving the healthy partner without the means to fund his or her core expenses. To qualify for Medicaid in most states, the healthy partner, called the "community spouse," can hold onto the house, one car and maximum financial assets of $115,920 in 2013 (although individual states can lower this amount to $23,184). If the community spouse or another dependent relative lives there, the house may be kept with no equity limit. If not, homes with equity values $536,000 to $802,000 (depending on state) may be retained when the owner accepts Medicaid for long-term care provided that the owner signs a form stating his or her intent to return to the house. Medicaid is then entitled to be reimbursed from the equity of the home when it is sold, generally after the recipient's death, so it is seldom worthwhile to pay real estate taxes, insurance and maintenance for a home owned by a long-term care Medicaid recipient.

The community spouse may also use all of the income in his or her name from pensions, Social Security, etc. and as much as $35,760 in income from the spouse in 2013 (which can be lowered by states). Income above this level must be applied toward nursing home expenses.

Although Medicaid laws and limits are given here for illustrative purposes only and are subject to change and interpretation, it does help explain the contention of many experts that there is a narrow window of wealth that should determine a couple's need for long-term care insurance. If non-home, non-car assets are below $115,920, Medicaid will kick in to fund the partner who needs long-term care. If non-home assets are above about $700,000, a couple can self-fund nearly all nursing home stays without depleting assets. It is those whose wealth ranges from about $150,000 to $700,000 who have the greatest need for long-term care insurance.

However, to avoid the possibility that a partner may survive for many years in a nursing home, ultimately draining more than $700,000, the best policy would be one that has a long elimination period, to reduce cost, but one that pays indefinitely. Currently the longest elimination period available on most policies is 365 days, but, irrationally, a very small proportion of buyers choose policies with elimination periods of more than 90 days.

Economists feel that the purpose of insurance is to pay for very expensive, but unlikely events and that we should self-insure against affordable but more likely events. This is analogous to upping the deductible on automobile collision insurance from $50, which causes the policy to be very expensive, to $500 or $1,000, which is much less expensive. According to the American Association for Long Term Care Insurance, "a policy that pays benefits for an unlimited amount of time costs only about a third more than the standard policy that pays for just 3 years of care.[30] You can even pay for nearly a third of that added cost by increasing the elimination period on your policy from the standard 90 days to 180 days. Now you're beginning to think like an economist – insure against the big losses you can't afford and don't sweat the small stuff.

In spite of paying expensive premiums for many years, some individuals who are "covered' by long term care insurance policies are surprised to find their claim denied by their insurance company. If you look at the fine print of a policy, you will find that eligibility is generally determined by one's inability to perform certain "activities of daily living." These include (1) bathing; (2) continence; (3) dressing; (4) eating; (5) toileting and (6) transferring (moving from one place to another). Before they pay benefits, most insurers require a physician to certify that you are unable to perform *two or more* of these activities,

48

although some policies specify an even greater number. To make things even more complex, many insurance companies will not pay unless you need hands-on assistance to perform an activity rather than stand-by assistance.

Bottom line, if you have long-term care insurance, look hard at its limitations and your own financial situation before you decide to continue paying its premiums (particularly if rates increase). If you don't have such insurance, carefully consider whether its likely benefits are worth the costs.

Partnership Policies

To help older Americans retain some of their needed assets if long-term care is needed, the federal Deficit Reduction Act of 2005 (DRA) created the Qualified State Long Term Care Partnership program. This program offers special long-term care policies that allow buyers to qualify for Medicaid when the policy runs out, and still hold on to some additional financial assets. The purpose of this Act is to provide incentives for people to buy long-term care insurance policies that will cover at least some of their long-term care needs, thereby saving the government some of their Medicaid expenses.

In most participating states, long-term care policy holders can keep a dollar in assets for every dollar that they have in long-term care coverage and still qualify for Medicaid. For example, if you have a 3-year policy that pays $150 a day, it would provide a total of $164,250 in benefits so you would be able to keep approximately $164 thousand and still qualify for Medicaid when you have spent your wealth down to that amount.

Don't forget that the greatest savings may result from having in an age-in-place home where an incapacitated spouse or single person may be able to live in a comfortable, familiar environment with some outside help for a long period of time at a fraction of the cost of a nursing home.

Continuing Care Retirement Communities

Continuing Care Retirement Communities (CCRCs) would appear to be an attractive option for many aging Americans. Generally situated in a campus-like setting, they offer to provide three levels of "life care,"[31] all within that community. At the first level, new residents live in independent homes and apartments much as they would if they lived independently outside of the continuing care community. The second level of care provides assisted living for those who need some help with the daily tasks of living. Finally, skilled nursing care is available for those with greater physical needs. The attractiveness of the communities is that once you buy in, you pay a set monthly fee for generally increasing levels of care for the rest of your life.

There were nearly 1,900 CCRCs in the US in the summer of 2009, mostly nonprofit organizations.[32] They are primarily regulated by states instead of the federal government. Buy-in deposits[33] for the all-inclusive "life care" range from $160,000 to $600,000 per person, depending upon location and the level of service. At the high end, chefs hired from gourmet restaurants provide the meals. Nationally, buy-in deposits average about a quarter of a million dollars per person.[34] Monthly fees average $2,500 to $5,400 per person.

While CCRCs have worked relatively well for decades, many have run into trouble in the wake of the financial crisis that began in 2008. By their very nature,

CCRCs lose some of their residents to death every year, and with high fixed costs, they must replace the monthly payments of those who die with new residents.[35] Many new residents have traditionally paid the high buy-in deposit by selling their homes. However, with the huge loss in home values beginning in 2008, this was no longer possible for some. In addition, some of the operating expenses of these facilities are paid by investment earnings from the buy-in fees, and lowered interest rates have greatly diminished this source of reliable income as well. Finally, some contracts call for a refund of the buy-in deposit when the resident dies, and without new residents moving in, the refunds drain the working capital needed to keep the operation going.

While it is unlikely that residents of CCRCs will have their life care terminated in the event that their community closes, residents may be moved to another, unfamiliar facility. More likely is a decline in the quality of service as operating income declines.

Many experts now feel that an investment in a CCRC is like any other risky investment and demands a close look at the finances of the company. Some states require that audited financial statements be given to prospective residents. Things to look for include:

• **Days of cash on hand** – which tells the number of days the facility can continue to operate without additional income. The average for CCRCs with one campus is 306 days of cash on hand; those with multiple sites average 281.

• **Cash-to-debt** should be about 35 percent. Typically, banks require 300 days of cash on hand and a minimum of 25 percent cash to debt. Be wary of facilities that are very dependent on investment income, donations or entry fees, since these facilities may not be able to run on income from operations alone.

• **Part of larger group**. Finally, it is useful to know if the facility is part of a larger group since other, failing communities could pull yours down as well.[36]

Bottom line; Continuing Care Retirement Communities can no longer be regarded as a type of annuity that is guaranteed to take care of your core retirement expenses for the rest of your life. Make sure that your deposit is refundable and is kept in escrow in the event that your community fails so that you can buy into another. Also, try to choose one in a state that regulates CCRCs very carefully and look over the financials carefully or have someone knowledgeable about finance do this for you before putting down a large part of your retirement assets.

Conclusion

In this book we present a retirement strategy that is much more traditional, and significantly safer than the balanced portfolios promoted by much of the financial industry. We feel that most people want a stream of income, guaranteed for life, which will enable them to continue living in comfort for the rest of their lives, no matter how long they live. This guaranteed lifetime income is provided to us by our Social Security retirement income as well as a defined benefit pension, if we are lucky enough to have one. The lifetime income stream that used to be provided through the defined benefit pension has now been largely replaced by defined contribution pensions such as 401(k) plans, which offer payments that are neither defined nor last a lifetime.

The cost of "living in comfort" is the ba *core* annual retirement expenses.   Our fun objective is to have at least enough core retiremen coming in every year of our lives to guarantee cov   .. .. our core retirement expenses.   If we have more than enough income to pay for our core expenses, we can even do totally discretionary things like build an estate, give large gifts to charity or try to get rich through our investment skills (or luck).   If we don't have enough guaranteed income to cover our core expenses for the rest of our lives, we can convert some of our assets into guaranteed lifetime income to try to close this gap.   The most efficient way to do this is through the purchase of an immediate fixed annuity.   If we still lack sufficient income to cover our core lifetime expenses, we must find the least unpleasant ways to cut back.   For most of us, this involves downsizing to a fully-paid off home in which we can age in place.   In many instances, a home of this type also enables us to avoid or minimize long-term care insurance which is becoming increasingly expensive.

While inflation has not been much of a problem in the US since the mid1980s, there is a good chance that it will come back again, hurting the standard of living of retirees with fixed incomes. Some types of lifetime income offer protection from inflation by adjusting automatically to increases in the cost of living.   These include Social Security retirement income, defined benefit pension income with cost of living adjustments (COLAs), and fixed annuity income which adjusts for inflation.   One of the best additional ways to protect against inflation is to minimize core expenses by owning much of what we need outright, including a low-maintenance, energy efficient home and a long-lasting car.   Inflation-protected income can be supplemented through the ownership of US Treasury

Inflation Protected Securities (TIPS) whose principal and interest adjust automatically to inflation, but at current low rates on Treasury bonds, this requires a relatively large investment to protect sources of income that are not adjusted for inflation.

Chapter 3
Annuity Equals Lifetime Security

At a Glance

If we do not have enough money coming in every year of our lives to guarantee coverage of our core retirement expenses, an annuity generally offers the most efficient way to close that gap. By "efficient," we mean that the appropriate annuity can give us a guaranteed annual payment for life that is *much* larger than any other type of investment. This is the big takeaway!

In addition to providing income that is guaranteed to last a lifetime, an annuity can also save us from mistakes that we might otherwise make as we age. Essentially an annuity can protect us against three important risks: *longevity risk* -- the risk of living longer than our life expectancy; *market risk* -- the risk that our income will fall if stock prices or interest rates go down; and what we might call *judgment risk* -- which is the risk that we, ourselves, might do something stupid to harm the lifetime income stream on which we depend.

But you have to be careful if you decide to use an annuity to close your lifetime income gap. There are all kinds of financial products out there that call themselves "annuities," many of which never end up paying a dollar in lifetime income. In this book we focus upon one particular type of annuity known as a Single Payment Immediate Annuity (SPIA). You begin by making a single upfront investment which is called a "premium" and generally receive a monthly income for life which begins a month after paying your premium. SPIAs are sold by most life insurance companies. Since payments are fixed, they eliminate *market risk*. Since they pay you for life, even if you live to be 105, they eliminate *longevity risk*. And since they *can't* be cashed in, they eliminate *judgment risk*. A few companies will sell them with inflation protection as well (at extra cost).

For those seeking to supplement their lifetime income, single payment immediate annuities offer the huge benefit of generating much more guaranteed income than any other type of investment. While a 70 year old man or a 73 year old woman could get a safe return of perhaps 2 ½ percent by investing in long-term US Treasury bonds, they could get a guaranteed annual cash flow of nearly 8 percent, or about *three times as much*, for life, by investing in a single payment immediate annuity. The highest payments are made to those who choose a "straight life" SPIA which makes payments only to a single person and nothing to his or her beneficiaries.

A downside of a straight life immediate annuity is that if you die soon after putting in your money, your estate gets nothing back. However, if your primary concern is protecting your own standard of living for life, this may not be an issue. It is possible to guarantee lifetime income from your annuity for a second person, perhaps a spouse, and it is also possible to guarantee payments to your heirs

56

for a certain number of years after you purchase the annuity, generally 5 or 10, if you die early. These added guarantees come at extra cost per monthly dollar of lifetime income.

Some people resist buying an immediate annuity because market interest rates are currently very low. This was one reason why my friend Phillip recently hesitated to buy one. While this concern is valid for the purchase of other fixed income products, such as bonds, it is far less important for immediate annuities since most of the guaranteed monthly cash flow is due to return of principal (the amount you put in), not to earnings on the investment. Later in this chapter we will demonstrate why it is probably not worthwhile waiting for rates to turn up before starting to buy some immediate annuities, if you need to supplement your lifetime income.

Life insurance companies that issue annuities are highly regulated by the states in which the policies are issued and are generally considered to be conservative and safe. States also have insurance funds to reimburse annuity holders in the very unlikely event that an insurance company fails. You can further protect yourself by diversifying annuity companies; i.e.: splitting your money between two or more highly rated providers.

Hopefully, some of you will learn by reading this chapter that an immediate fixed annuity is just what you need to close your lifetime income gap. However, you may lack the financial assets needed to buy this annuity. For those of you who own your own age-in-place homes in which you plan to live out the rest of your lives, the good news is that a *reverse mortgage* may allow you to live in your current home for the rest of your life and also receive guaranteed lifetime monthly income through an annuity funded by this mortgage. Reverse mortgages will be discussed in more detail later in this chapter.

Why Economists Like Annuities

How would you like to have a guaranteed income coming to you each month for the rest of your life, regardless of how long you live or what dumb mistakes you may end up making along the way? This is what an annuity can do for you.

If this looks familiar, it should, since it is what we get from Social Security as well as from a traditional "defined benefit" pension if we are lucky enough to have one. Both are forms of annuities because both pay for life. Virtually every economist who studies retirement issues feels that annuities are generally the best way to close a lifetime income gap. In fact, economists are very surprised that relatively few retirees choose to invest at least some of their savings in a life annuity. They even have a name for this strange behavior which they call the "annuity puzzle."[37]

In his Nobel Prize acceptance speech, Professor Franco Modigliani of MIT said:

"It is a well-known fact that annuity contracts, other than in the form of group insurance through pension systems, are extremely rare. Why this should be so is a subject of considerable current interest. It is still ill-understood." [38]

According to Professor Jeffrey R. Brown, often regarded as the leading scholar of annuities:

"The empirical evidence on annuitization suggests that individuals do not behave as if they value annuities as highly as theory would predict. This is evidenced by the fact that the private market for immediate annuities or payout annuities was only $11.8 billion in 2005."[39] And part of this tiny amount included annuities that paid out for only a certain number of years as opposed to the life annuities favored by economists. In fact, so few Americans

58

have a privately-purchased life annuity that they barely show up on widespread national surveys such as the Survey of Consumer Finances or the Health and Retirement Study (HRS).

Annuities are attractive to most economists because they insure us against living *too long.*[40] According to the Social Security Administration, a 70 year old American man will live, on average, 13.73 years while a 70 year old woman will live, on average, 16.05 years. If the 70 year old man had $100,000 in savings, perhaps from a 401(k) or IRA, and he invested it safely in Treasury bonds or bank CD's which paid 2 percent per year, he could withdraw $8,401 per year for his remaining (on average) 13.73 years to help pay for his retirement. The woman could withdraw $7,346 for 16.05 years. However, at the end of that time, they would have nothing left of their nest egg in the event that they live longer, and half are expected to do just that.

The magic of an annuity is that if everyone participated and we pooled together all of that money, we could guarantee that both the man and the woman would continue to receive *that exact same amount* for the rest of their lives, no matter how long they lived. Instead of getting $8,401 per year for just 13.73 years from an investment in Treasury bonds at 2 percent interest, the 70 year old man in our example would get $8,401 per year *for the rest of his life,* even if he lived to be 110![41] It doesn't sound possible.

The secret of annuities is that in exchange for getting the same amount that you'd get without an annuity, but for *life*, none of your investment goes to your heirs. At the extreme, if you bought a life annuity at age 70 for $200,000 and you died the next day; your estate would get nothing. Had you *not* bought the annuity and put your money into bank CD's, your estate would get $200,000.

So, if you are a single person with no heirs, an annuity looks like a pretty good deal. And rest assured that even if you had a spouse or children to whom you wanted to leave some of your income or wealth, you could get an annuity which would pay *you* less money each year for your life but could pay your surviving spouse for the rest of his or her life as well or leave some money to your kids. But these are complications that we will deal with later.

Aside from providing income for life, a second major benefit of an immediate annuity, for those who worry about being swindled in their dotage by an unscrupulous investment salesman or a new spouse, is that *most are virtually unswindleable!* Once you pay the money, you are going to get a monthly check for the rest of your life, period. This is why an immediate annuity is sometimes called a "non-refund" annuity – once your single deposit premium is paid, you generally can't get your money back, discouraging most swindlers. When they learn that your assets have been invested in an SPIA, they'll move on, instead, to the next vulnerable old-timer.

To some, the purchase of an immediate annuity looks unattractive because it reduces their liquidity or ability to get their hands on their $200,000 (or whatever they paid) once they have bought the annuity. What if someone comes along with a great deal on land in Nevada or what if one of the kids needs $50,000 to buy a house or a business or send a grandkid to college? You would no longer be able to say "yes." Is this a downside or an upside of an annuity?

If you are thinking about investing in an immediate annuity, at least partially because you can't change your mind if your mental acuity diminishes (or if someone preys on your weakness to get at those funds), make sure that the annuity that you choose does *NOT* offer you a liquidity option that will let you cash it in.

Some of the insurance companies that, at the time of this writing, appeared to protect you against yourself by making it impossible to cash in an SPIA include:

Allianz
American Equity
American General
Jackson National
Kansas City Life
Midland National
Minnesota Life Insurance Company
North American
Symetra

This list is not inclusive and it may not be up-to-date. If the lack of liquidity is a feature that appeals to you, double check to be sure that the company that you choose offers you this safeguard.

An annuity works because the organization that pools the money (which could be an insurance company, your employer or Social Security) has a large number of people in the pool and has a pretty good guess of the average life expectancy of everyone in the pool. For every person who lives longer than his or her life expectancy and collects extra payments, someone lives shorter than life expectancy and gives up those payments. It is the job of the organization's statisticians or "actuaries" to estimate the life expectancy of those in the pool. Note that different pools may have different kinds of people with different life expectancies.

The biggest pool is run by Social Security since nearly every American worker must belong to it. However, if you belong to a pool of college professors, like myself, who do little dangerous work or heavy lifting and tend to eat well and not smoke, its members will have a longer life expectancy than the average worker in the Social Security pool and an even greater life expectancy than National

Football League players, many of whom have been found to suffer life-shortening effects of head injuries. As a result, the same $200,000 will buy those in a pool of college professors a smaller monthly payment for life, because they are expected to live so long, and will buy former football players a greater monthly payment because of their shorter life expectancy.

Immediate Fixed Annuities

Please don't rush out right now to buy an annuity from the first salesperson you run into. There are a few more things you need to know to keep from wasting your money on the wrong kind of annuity. The kind of annuity that I am talking about is the *single payment immediate annuity*, the most basic type, where you pay in a sum of money and get a fixed monthly payment for life.

Chances are that the salesperson will try to talk you into buying a "variable annuity." The world "variable" means that it does not give you the same guaranteed monthly amount of money for life. It also tends to be far more profitable for the insurance company that issues it and for the salesman who sells it! With the ability to defer paying taxes on money invested in variable annuities, they may be reasonable investments for younger, working people in high tax brackets and a willingness to take on risk. However, they are generally terrible investments for retired people whose tax brackets have fallen and who generally try to avoid risk.

If you put your $200,000 into a variable annuity, you are generally buying risky stocks and bonds rather than an ironclad payment for the rest of your life. Yes, you can arrange to get a payment for the rest of your life, but the amount of the payment depends largely on how well your investments do. If the stock market collapses, as it did in 2008, loosing half its value, and if your variable annuity is

invested in stocks or a stock mutual fu
possibly see your monthly payment fall sub
variable annuity is invested in a *target d*
you can be in real trouble since target date
rebalance your money away from safe asse
into even more risky assets, like stocks, as the stock mar
falls. (Incidentally, those who sign up for a 401k at work
and don't specify how their money should be invested must
be put into a target date fund, by default.)

The companies that market variable annuities make
money in two ways – from selling you an insurance policy
which may guarantee a certain *minimum* payment for life,[42]
and from selling you the mutual fund into which the
variable portion of your money is invested. Some variable
annuities are very expensive, with upfront fees of 2 to 5
percent and annual fees that can run to 2 or 3 percent (or
more) of the amount invested. In a low-earning investment
environment, like the one we have seen over most of the
past 13 years, this can amount to a large part (or all) of your
total return. There are less expensive variable annuities, if
you really want one and are willing to shop around.

Deferred Fixed Annuities

An even cheaper way of buying guaranteed lifetime
income which pays off if you live longer than your life
expectancy, is to put off or defer the income for a few years
by buying a deferred fixed annuity. Here, a 70 year old
man in good physical and mental health whose parents
lived into their mid-80s or even 90s might buy a fixed
annuity now which doesn't begin to make payments until
an advanced age such as 85. This is considered to be true
longevity insurance because it only pays off if you live past
a specified old age.

Why would the 70 year old pay his money now but
put off receiving income for 15 years? The answer is that a

erred fixed annuity is much cheaper than an immediate
ixed annuity. While a 70 year old man could purchase an
annual payment of $16,802 for life for $200,000, if he was
willing to wait to age 85 to begin receiving the same
$16,802 per year, his cost right now would be only
$66,075, or about a third of the $200,000 cost of having
payments begin immediately. This smaller payment is due
to two things. First his life expectancy at age 85 will be
much less than it is now, just 5.65 years.[43] This means that
he needs a much smaller investment at age 85[44] than at age
70 to pay for an annuity of $16,802.35 per year. Second,
the $66,075 he puts in now will grow at interest for 15
years, enlarging the amount that can be used for his payout.

The primary purpose of buying a deferred fixed
annuity is to get pure longevity insurance to protect
yourself against living too long. This is useful for those of
us who have sufficient income to cover our core expenses
for the rest of our *expected* lives, but not enough to cover
those expenses if we beat the odds and live longer than our
life expectancy. If you buy a policy that only begins to
make payments at your current life expectancy age (say 85
for a man now 70), you can avoid buying additional annual
payments for your *expected* lifetime (from 70 to 85), which
makes it much cheaper. If you live longer than 85, you can
get annual payments of $16,802.35 for as long as you live
for a payment now (when you are 70) of $66,075 as we just
saw, above.

Not only does a deferred annuity give you greater
flexibility with your assets than you would have with an
immediate annuity, but you also will leave something to
your beneficiaries if you die before age 85. Also, and this
is important, if you have sufficient core income to last for
the next 15 years, you avoid the investment associated with
buying an annuity to cover those years. There is also a tax
advantage to buying a deferred fixed annuity in that the

interest earned after you buy the annuity and before you begin to take it out is tax-deferred until you begin taking payments.   Since there is no limit to the amount that you can put into a deferred annuity, it may be a useful vehicle for those in a high tax bracket to tax-defer earnings on their investments.

However, there are some drawbacks to a *deferred* fixed annuity. If you don't shop very carefully, you will find that they may have a lot of fees not typically found in the simpler immediate fixed annuity. Some policies may have a *front-end sales charge* which is an upfront fee or "load" generally used to compensate the salesperson who sold you the annuity. These days, most companies have done away with this charge although Vanguard recently told me that they have a one-time transaction fee of 2 percent already included in the quote. If there is a load, it could be a fixed load, as in the case of Vanguard at 2 percent, or a sliding load, where the percentage goes down as the size of the policy increases.

A more worrisome aspect is the fact that nearly all deferred fixed annuities allow you to surrender or cash in your contract after you have paid in your money but before the first lifetime payment is made. This leaves a long period of increasing vulnerability in which you can be "convinced" to surrender your policy which can deprive you of lifetime annual income if you live past your life expectancy. If you do surrender your policy, or withdraw a partial amount, you generally have to pay a *surrender charge*. Most fixed deferred annuities allow withdrawals of up to 10 percent of the balance each year without penalty, but any withdrawal above this amount is subject to the surrender charge which generally starts high but declines each year after purchase. As an example, there may be a 5 percent charge on money taken out the first year, decreasing to 4 percent the second year and so on until it is zero at the end of 5 years. As you can see, the fees are hardly substantial enough to keep someone from attempting to persuade you to cash out your policy and give the money to them.

Many life insurance companies offer competitive rates on deferred fixed annuities, partly because they like having control of your money for a long period of time. When you begin calling companies to get a quote, tell them the age when you plan to purchase the deferred annuity and the age when you would like to begin receiving fixed payments for life. It is a good idea to first price the "plain vanilla" product, which is for a single life (your own) with no "bells and whistles" such as a five or 10 year guarantee or return of premiums if you die before you begin receiving payments. The beauty of getting this quote is that any front end fees and expenses are already embedded in it so you can compare "apples to apples." Whoever offers you the best rate on the plain vanilla product is also likely to offer you the best rate on the bells and the whistles, if you feel that you need them.

Cost of a Fixed Annuity

The cost of buying a guaranteed income for life through a fixed annuity, whether immediate or deferred, depends on four things.
1. Your gender
2. The interest rate paid by the insurance company
3. The average life expectancy of those in your pool
4. The expenses charged to you by the insurance company

Gender and Annuity Cost

On average, women live longer than men. At age 65, women will tend to live an average of 20.12 more years while men will average just another 16.8 years, which is 3.32 years less than women. Percentagewise, 65 year old women live nearly 20 percent longer than 65 year old men.

Since women are expected to live longer than men, it is not surprising that the cost for an annuity that pays a set amount per month for life (say $1,000) should cost more for a woman than for a man because women are expected to receive that monthly flow of money for several additional years. For that reason, nearly all annuities are sold on a gender-specific basis to reflect life expectancy.

While this may appear to some to reflect discrimination against women, it is regarded as both legal and fair in 49 states. As of 2013, only one state, Montana, insists that annuities be sold on a unisex basis which uses average life expectancy of people of both genders for everyone. This makes the cost for a dollar of lifetime income higher for men and lower for women than it would be in the other 49 states.[45] As of the time this book was written, the Montana legislature was considering the elimination of unisex annuity provisions. The reason for the repeal probably has to do with the fact that few men in that state would consider buying a unisex annuity since it would cost them considerably more than in other states, and the women in Montana might not find unisex policies to be all that attractive either since insurance companies would have to charge more to all annuity purchasers because the great majority of buyers would be bargain-seeking, longer-living women.

Interest Rate

When you make an upfront purchase of a fixed annuity, the insurance company invests your money in secure assets so that the money will be available when it has to be paid out. The more interest they can earn on your money, the more they can pay out to you. Therefore, it would be useful for you to know the interest rate that the insurance company is willing to pay on your annuity.

Unfortunately, this is often difficult, if not impossible to find out. Rather than show the actual interest rate, which these days is often just a percent or two, they tend to quote annuities in terms of monthly or annual payments that they will make to you, for life, if you invest a certain amount of money. Since much of the payment is return of your principal, rather than interest, the shorter your life expectancy, the greater the payment for each dollar invested. Some companies multiply the monthly payment by 12 and divide the annual payment by the amount invested, calling this rate the "annual payout rate" or "cash flow." Since the annual payout rate is given in percent form, many consumers will confuse it with the interest rate the company will actually pay you which finance professionals call the "internal rate of return" or "IRR."

The first place to go to find out the monthly lifetime income that you can generate with an investment in an immediate annuity is www.immediateannuities.com. This web site, which enables you to get quotes anonymously, will ask you your age, your gender, the amount you want to invest and the state in which you live and will then give you the greatest amount of lifetime income offered by a dozen or more companies. In July, 2013, an investment of $1 million in a single life policy for a 70 year old man, with no payments made to beneficiaries, would pay $6,526 per month which is $78,312 per year. The "annual payout rate" is shown as 7.83 percent per year since it is about 7.83 percent of one million dollars. Compare this to the 2.5 percent return on 10 year Treasury notes offered at the same time and you can see why an immediate annuity is so appealing.

If you know the life expectancy of 70 year old men

(13.73 years according to Social Security tables), the annual payment ($78,312) and the amount invested ($1 million), you can calculate the actual interest rate that is being paid to you by the insurance company (the "internal rate of return") which is 1 percent.[46] This is just barely an eighth of the 7.83 percent "annual payout rate" that is quoted so prominently. The other 7/8ths of your annual payment is a *return of your own money*.

I often get offers from universities I attended or charities to which I contributed, offering me lifetime payments which, depending on my age, appear to pay me 6, 7, or even 8 percent on my contribution. Of course, this is the annual payout rate, not the actual interest rate, which is likely to be far lower than that offered by the best quote in immediateannuities.com. The reason for this is that the university or charity wants there to be something left over for them when I die.

To see the relative unimportance of current interest rates in annuities, Table 1 estimates how much men and women of various ages would get annually from an immediate annuity if they invested $200,000. Many readers will be surprised to see that large changes in interest rates don't have such a huge impact on payments. This is because we are not talking about a large number of years in which compounding can do its magic (life expectancy of older people) and because money that is paid out to you stops earning interest. For a man aged 70, for example, a *doubling* of the interest rate from 1 percent to 2 percent moves lifetime annual payments from $15,662.12 to $16,802.35, an increase of just 7.3 percent. This observation will come into play when we consider whether it is worth waiting for interest rates to increase before investing in an annuity. The short answer is "no." It turns out that my pediatrician friend Phillip was right and I was wrong. This is not a bad time

Life Expectancy of Pool

Unfortunately, no private company is willing to write an annuity for us based on the Social Security life expectancy table. All of the insurance companies want to believe that we are going to live longer than the average American so they offer to pay out less over our lifetimes than the tables would appear to warrant. Why is this the case?

First, people who have the money and knowledge to buy an annuity are not average; they tend to be richer and better educated. Richer and better educated people tend to

Table 1
Annual Payments for an Investment of $200,000
In an Immediate Fixed Annuity with Different Interest Rates

Age Men	Life Expectancy	1%	2%	3%	4%	5%	6%
60	20.92	$10,642.62	$11,793.21	$13,010.16	$14,291.14	$15,633.46	$17,034.08
65	17.19	$12,721.24	$13,863.88	$15,061.30	$16,311.94	$17,614.03	$18,965.61
70	13.73	$15,662.12	$16,802.35	$17,986.43	$19,213.35	$20,481.96	$21,791.02
75	10.62	$19,944.01	$21,090.14	$22,270.19	$23,483.46	$24,729.25	$26,006.78
Women							
60	23.97	$9,425.13	$10,584.56	$11,819.64	$13,127.25	$14,503.73	$15,944.95
65	19.89	$11,138.46	$12,286.48	$13,497.67	$14,769.96	$16,100.92	$17,487.86
70	16.05	$13,549.87	$14,691.02	$15,883.38	$17,125.57	$18,416.05	$19,753.12
75	12.55	$17,036.61	$18,177.85	$19,359.18	$20,579.73	$21,838.53	$23,134.54

Life expectancy based on Social Security Period Life Table 2007

be healthier and live longer. If the insurance company wrote annuities assuming that 70 year old male annuity buyers would live just 13.73 years, which is the average life expectancy for all American 70 year old men, they would lose money because those who want to buy annuities tend to live longer than average.

Second, even among those who have the money and knowledge to buy annuities, those who choose to do so are often making a sly bet – they have good reason to believe that they will live longer than their life expectancies. How do they know this? For one thing, they are currently in good health with no problems or illnesses associated with early death. For another thing, they are often children of parents who lived long lives and longevity tends to be at least partially genetic. Third, they probably are not daredevils who race motorcycles, do helicopter skiing or engage in reckless sex.

I was once on a business trip with a very bright man in his late 50s who told me that he was not going to annuitize any of his pension income. When I asked him why, he told me that neither of his parents lived to be 60 and that, for him, an annuity was a bad bet.

The tendency of people to buy insurance policies only if they think it will pay off handsomely for them is known in the industry as "adverse selection." Since we insurance or annuity buyers have the edge of self-knowledge over the sellers, we tilt the odds of a good payoff in our favor and force the sellers to raise the price to compensate.

For some 30 years of my life, I owned and flew small airplanes. Not being a particularly good pilot (although I am still alive), I knew that my life expectancy was lower than other men of my age and occupation (college professor). Therefore, whenever I was offered the opportunity to buy life insurance through work at a good price, I looked to see if private pilots were excluded. In most cases they were, since we had a higher risk of collecting on the policies (actually, it would have been our families who collected). Occasionally, I was surprised to learn that they didn't exclude private pilots, probably since few college professors participate in this hobby. In that

71

case, I would buy additional life insurance, using the process of adverse selection to my advantage (even though it never paid off).

In some cases, insurance companies can examine us individually to reduce the effect of adverse selection. For example, if we want to buy a large *life* insurance policy, they will generally demand that we come in for a physical to be sure that we don't have cancer or a heart condition that would force them to pay out early. The companies don't generally do this for buyers of annuities and adjust for adverse selection by putting us in different pools. However, one insurance company rep that I talked to said that if I could show that I had a serious illness or other life-shortening condition, they could give me a better deal on my annuity.

Recently, I called my pension company, TIAA-CREF, which specializes in defined contribution pensions and insurance for college professors and teachers, to inquire about purchasing an immediate annuity. The quote that I got was based upon a 3 percent rate of interest (return on investment) to which I was entitled on money that had long been in my account. Therefore, when I told them how much I wanted to invest and they told me how much I would get per month for the rest of my life, I was able to calculate the life expectancy they assigned to me at age 70. This was 15.27 years which is 1.54 years more than the Social Security table for all Americans. As you can see, my insurance company assumed that I would live more than 10 percent longer than the average 70 year old American guy. And the only things they really knew about me, to make me different, was that I was better educated than most, worked in a job that didn't grind down my body or knock my brains around, and *wanted to buy an annuity*. They didn't even ask if I was a mediocre private pilot which would have tilted the odds more in their favor.

Expenses Associated with Annuities

It costs money for companies to issue annuities, and these expenses will be passed along to you, the buyer. Some companies have small expenses, leaving most of the earnings to you, while others have large expenses, capable of eating up what little you can earn. The expenses can be divided into four basic categories which I will call administrative, aggregate longevity risk, marketing and profit.

Administrative expenses include writing policies, making payments, setting rates and holding reserves, among other things. Insurance companies are unique in that they must hire or pay for the services of actuaries who are very highly paid statisticians, trained to examine large amounts of data to help set rates on the company's products. Insurance companies are also somewhat unique in that they are regulated by state insurance commissions who insist that they hold reserves that are *more than adequate* to make expected payouts. This is because the companies' annuity holders may strangely end up living far longer than anticipated, causing the company to take a loss on this group. Life insurance companies also pay their top officers very well. A recent survey of the largest 10 publicly-traded life insurers found that median salaries for CEOs were $6 million per year while those of chairmen were even higher at $7.3 million. [47]

There is another type of possible expense that the insurance companies take on when they write annuities. This is the expense attached to "aggregate longevity risk" or the risk that some unforeseen medical breakthrough is going to cause the life expectancy of those with annuities to jump, thereby lengthening the payments that they must make. If increases in longevity are predictable, as most are, the insurance company and its actuaries can build this into the pricing. However, a new pill that allows people to lose 25 pounds without effort is hard to predict and some allowance has to be built into the pricing for that possibility.

Thus far, the expenses we have discussed are similar for most insurance companies and will not cause expenses to differ drastically among them. Where they do differ significantly is in the cost of marketing and in profitability. For example, annuities that are sold individually by salesmen are naturally going to be more expensive than those sold in group form or individually over the internet or by phone.

Most insurance companies are owned by shareholders who expect them to make a profit. This profit is generally built into the rates charged on annuities which diminish your payout per dollar invested. There are not-for-profit insurance companies that offer annuities as well, and these may be less expensive than the for-profit companies, but not necessarily so since many large not-for-profit firms also pay huge salaries to their officers and offer great benefits and facilities for their employees.

Single payment immediate annuities are often sold with relatively low profit margins for the companies that offer them. Economists consider most single payment immediate annuities to be "commodities" which are nearly identical products offered by many companies at very similar prices. SPIAs are a relatively "simple" product whose expected cost to the insurance company is based on annuity tables that are virtually identical for most companies. Therefore, the investment a consumer must make to produce a given monthly cash flow for life depends almost entirely on a person's age and gender. For that reason, it is relatively easy to shop for them by comparing the monthly payment ("Cash Flow") for the investment you are willing to make. A web site such as immediateannuities.com has calculators that will give you (anonymously) the best monthly payment quote offered in your state by a company who pays to be part of the commercial web site. As we will see shortly, these may be for-profit companies whose costs could be higher than some not-for-profits who may not be listed on the site. However, it is useful to get quotes from these web sites as well before you make your decision. Just Google "single payment immediate annuity quote" to find these sites. It is worthwhile checking the quotes from not-for-profit companies that may not be included in the comparative web sites. Some not-for-profits who tend to offer good rates on annuities include TIAA-CREF, particularly for members, USAA which serves primarily those who serve or have served in the military and their families, and Vanguard, which works with insurance companies but is known for low fees.

Social Security Annuity Deal

The best annuity deal in America, by far, is offered to those under the age of 70 by Social Security. At a time when the return on 10 year Treasury bonds is barely over 2 percent, unadjusted for inflation, and the return on 10 year Treasury bonds adjusted for inflation (TIPS) is close to zero or below,[48] you can get a boost of 8 percent on your Social Security retirement earnings, fully adjusted for inflation, by delaying the start of your payments by a year[49].

"Full" Social Security Retirement Benefits are available to those who reach "Full Retirement Age," which varies between 66 and 67 depending on your year of birth. Table 2 gives full retirement age by year of birth.

If you retire between age 62 and your full retirement age, your retirement benefits are reduced, often substantially. For example, those born between 1943 and 1954 whose full retirement age is 66 lose 25 percent of this amount if they retire at age 62. However, if that same person retires between full retirement age and age 70, his or

Table 2
Age of Full Social Security Benefits

Year of Birth	Full Retirement Age
On or before 1954	66
1955	66 and 2 months
1956	66 and 4 months
1957	66 and 6 months
1958	66 and 8 months
1959	66 and 10 months
1960 or later	67

Source: Social Security Retirement Planner: Delayed Retirement Credits http://www.socialsecurity.gov/retire2/delayret.htm

her Social Security retirement benefits are *increased* by 8 percent per year. If, for example, your full retirement age is 66 and you hold off taking your benefits until your 70th birthday, your (inflation-adjusted) Social Security Retirement Benefits will be increased by 32 percent. Your only risk is the chance that you will die before taking any of your benefits at age 70.

However, the risk that you will die between ages 66 and 70 are very low, making the 8 percent real return a better and better deal. According to the Social Security life expectancy tables, a 66 year old man has a 1.8 percent chance of dying before his next birthday. This probability increases slightly to 2 percent for 67 year olds, 2.1 percent for 68 year olds and 2.3 percent for 69 year olds, an average of just over 2 percent per year for those men age 66 to 70. Probability of death is even lower for women, making it an even better deal for them. And given what we have learned about adverse selection, for healthy

76

individuals who expect to live a long time, this deal is hard to pass up, even if you have to use some of your savings to supplement your income until you begin to collect Social Security at age 70.

In spite of the benefits offered by Social Security to delay the start of payments in exchange for a larger lifetime annuity payment, very few workers take advantage of them. Professor Brown reports:

"While individuals are permitted to claim Social Security benefits as early as age 62, they are not required to do so. Individuals who delay claiming are essentially purchasing (at better than market prices) a larger inflation-indexed annuity for the future. Research on benefit claiming behavior, however, suggests that very few individuals avail themselves of this opportunity, with only one out of ten men retiring before their sixty-second birthday delaying benefits claiming for at least a year."[50] This has to be considered another part of the "annuity puzzle."

Professor Brown cites results from the government's Health and Retirement Survey where a large proportion of respondents indicated that they would trade in their lifetime Social Security retirement benefits for a lump sum payment whose actuarial value was less than or equal to those offered by Social Security. He concludes:

"Clearly, if a large share of respondents are willing to give up the best annuity they own for a lump sum that is less than or equal to the actuarially fair level, then these individuals are not behaving as if they place a high insurance value on the annuity."[51]

The greatest proportion of workers (about 44 percent) begin to take their Social Security retirement benefits at age 62 followed by about 27 percent who take them at the full retirement age of 66. Hardly anyone waits past age 66 in spite of the fact that the inflation-adjusted returns offered to workers who are willing and able to wait are incredible and unavailable anywhere else. Unless you expect to die soon or just can't do without your Social Security money for a few more years, it is foolish to start taking your Social Security payments before your 70th birthday. I waited until my 70th birthday and boy am I happy!

Tax Considerations of Annuities

If you buy an immediate fixed annuity with after-tax dollars, you will find that your taxes on these payments will be negligible for two reasons. First, most of the payment that you receive is merely a return of your own investment on which you've already paid taxes. Second, today's very low interest rate environment means that the annuity is not generating much in the way of taxable income.

To illustrate, let's consider the example from earlier in the chapter which was taken from the best quote shown on the web site *www.immediateannuities.com*. According to the quote, a 70 year old man would get an annual payment of $79,573 on an investment of $1,000,000. If he used *pre-tax* funds to buy this, say, from an IRA, a 401(k), etc., it would *all* be taxable since he has never paid any taxes at all on these earnings.

If, however, he funded it with after-tax dollars, the portion of each payment which is the return of the after-tax money he invested is not taxable. This percentage is called the "exclusion ratio." It is calculated by multiplying the annual payment by a multiple supplied by the IRS which loosely corresponds to the life expectancy of both men and women, to arrive at the "expected return" and then dividing the cost of the policy by the expected return.

The IRS multiple at age 70 (for both men and women) is 16.[52] Multiply this by the annual payment of

$79,573 and you get $1,273,168 which is the amount that the annuity buyer could expect to receive over a 16 year lifetime. If you divide this into the $1 million cost of the annuity you will find that $1,000,000/$1,273,168 = 78.54 percent of every payment is not taxed. Stated another way, you must only pay tax on 21.46 percent of what you receive from the annuity, which is an estimate of the interest. If you are in the 25 percent marginal federal tax bracket, you would only pay 5.37 percent (25 percent of 21.46 percent) on your annuity payments.

Note that once you have reached the life expectancy calculated by the IRS and have received payments equal to your investment; every additional payment received is fully taxable. It is also important to realize that if you purchase an immediate annuity with savings from a regular (non-Roth) IRA, *all* of your payments will be taxable since taxes had never been paid on the income used to accumulate the IRA.

Covering RMD with Annuity Payments

If you have accumulated pre-tax income in a 401(k), a Keogh Plan, an IRA or other type of defined contribution pension plan, by law you must begin withdrawing money from that plan at age 70 ½, and paying income taxes on the full amount of your withdrawal. The Required Minimum Distribution (RMD) is specified in a table provided by the IRS and is based on a "distribution period" which is far longer than actuarial life expectancy. This is shown in Table 2, below. The first year withdrawal at age 70 is 3.65 percent of your pre-tax accumulation, and this goes up slowly every year for the rest of your life.

Table 3
Required Minimum Distribution

Age	Distribution Period	Required Distribution
70	27.4	3.65%
71	26.5	3.77%
72	25.6	3.91%
73	24.7	4.05%
74	23.8	4.20%
75	22.9	4.37%
76	22	4.55%
77	21.2	4.72%
78	20.3	4.93%
79	19.5	5.13%
80	18.7	5.35%
81	17.9	5.59%
82	17.1	5.85%
83	16.3	6.13%
84	15.5	6.45%
85	14.8	6.76%
86	14.1	7.09%
87	13.4	7.46%
88	12.7	7.87%
89	12	8.33%
90	11.4	8.77%

You can use your accumulated pre-tax income to purchase an immediate annuity that will pay out an annual amount sufficient to cover your RMD. However, since income taxes have never been paid on these dollars, the RMD payments are fully taxable.

If, however, all of your pre-tax retirement accumulations are used to purchase a Single Payment Immediate Annuity (SPIA), there is a special IRS provision that says that the payout on the annuity (all of which is taxable) will satisfy your Required Minimum Distributions on that accumulation for life. This means that you will get income for life from your annuity and will not have to worry about withdrawing the appropriate amount of RMD each year, even though the RMD keeps getting larger. Since both the annuity and the RMD are based on life expectancy tables, the IRS allows for this simplification. In fact, this ruling applies even if you purchase an annuity that increases payments by as much as 5 percent per year (to offset expected inflation), or that increases automatically with the cost of living. You may note that if you take advantage of the IRS rule that allows your annuity payments to substitute for your RMD, you will have to pay more taxes earlier on. Using our traditional example, a 70 year old man will receive about 6.8 percent of the amount he invested in an SPIA per year for life. Using the RMD table we learn that he is only required to take out (and pay taxes on) 3.65 percent of his accumulation at age 70 if he doesn't have it in an annuity. In fact, it isn't until past age 85 that he has to withdraw as much as the 6.8 percent he gets from his annuity. Therefore, from a tax perspective, annuitizing the entire amount of the untaxed retirement accumulation may not be wise. Check with your tax advisor before making your decision.

Remember, if you use only part of your pre-tax retirement accumulation to purchase an SPIA, (keeping some aside, perhaps for purposes of liquidity) you are responsible for calculating your RMD from the full pre-tax retirement accumulation each year.

Annuities with Inflation-Protection

Unfortunately, it is getting more difficult and expensive to find an annuity that will protect you against unanticipated inflation, which is the kind that can hurt! Up until a few years ago, many insurance companies sold immediate "fixed" annuities that were fixed in "real" terms, which means that they were adjusted for the actual cost of living. These days, if you want a fixed annuity with a cost of living adjustment, many companies will try to sell you, instead, an annuity that increases payments by a fixed amount each year, such as 3 percent, 4 percent or 5 percent. It is up to *you* to guess what the rate of inflation will be and you will end up paying more for an annuity with a "cost-of-living" adjustment, the additional amount depending on the percentage increase you want to buy.

Inflation-protected annuities are more difficult to find these days for two reasons. First, the insurance companies that may issue them are forced by their financially conservative regulators to find an asset that will take away their risk in the event that inflation spikes upward. While they could invest the funds in safe, inflation-protected securities such as TIPS, whose pattern (technically "duration") of payments matches that of the annuity, TIPS currently pay extremely low real interest rates which can be zero or even negative.[53] This means that inflation-protected annuities must offer much less initial annual income for a given investment (or charge a much greater amount for a comparable cash flow) than annuities without inflation protection and will appear unattractive to many consumers.

In 2010, before returns on TIPS fell so substantially, Vanguard offered an inflation-protected annuity that was regarded as being very competitive. Even then, however, their initial payments were approximately 20 to 30 percent

82

lower than the payments received from a regular, non-inflation-protected immediate annuity[54]. Although inflation would probably even out the payments in less than 10 years, this huge initial difference in payments appeared to have reduced demand significantly.

I recently received a quote on a single premium immediate fixed annuity with a consumer price index (CPI) adjustment. It was offered by American General Life Insurance Company, a highly rated company. First, the good news! The CPI adjustment for inflation was based on the CPI-U which is the all urban consumer price index that includes retirees. This is better for retirees than the current CPI used by Social Security, the CPI-W, which includes only workers who have different needs than retirees (they use less health care, on average, for example). This quote also guarantees that the chained index, proposed by President Obama, will not be used. The chained index also works against the retiree who cannot substitute other, cheaper goods, when medical costs go up.

For an investment of $100,000 at age 70 and 2 months, the annuity promised to pay me $436.72 per month for the rest of my life, fully adjusted for inflation. This comes to $5,241 per year which is sometimes shown as an annual cash flow of 5.24 percent. They also gave me a quote of $595.72 per month ($7,149 per year) for the rest of my life for an annuity that offered no cost of living protection. Therefore, an investment of $100,000 will pay me $159 less per month if I want the inflation protection. On a base of $436.72 per month from the annuity which adjusts to the cost of living, giving up the inflation protection will give me $159/$436.72 or 36.4 percent more.

It is possible to calculate the inflation rate needed to have these two quotes break even over my life expectancy. To do this however, I need to know what the insurer expects my life expectancy to be. If they use the Social

Security life expectancy table, I would be expected to live about 13 more years which would mean that average inflation would have to be more than about 4.1 percent per year to make me better off with the inflation-adjusted policy. However, as noted elsewhere in this book, folks who buy annuities expect to live longer than others, so my quote undoubtedly reflects a higher life expectancy than that given by Social Security for all 70 year olds. If it were 15 years rather than 13 years, the break-even inflation rate would be 3.87 percent, a shade under the 4.1 percent shown above for a shorter life expectancy. [55]

In any event, the results are clear. Unless I expect that inflation will go from the current level of about 2 percent to well above 4 percent during my remaining years, (in order to average just below 4 percent), I would be better off declining the inflation adjustment. However, if I felt that inflation during my remaining lifetime is likely to be much above the level of the past century (3.43 percent) perhaps as high or higher than the highest 30 year inflation in the post-WWII period (5.44 percent), the deal offered by American General is not a bad way to hedge. If I am risk-averse and worry that possible high rates of inflation can endanger my comfortable standard of living in retirement, this deal is worth serious consideration.

Alternative Inflation Protection

Since few if any insurance companies are willing to take on the risk of unanticipated inflation without charging extra to do so, you may wish to do it yourself. There are two ways in which you can do this, both of which involve investing in Treasury Inflation-Protected Securities (TIPS). TIPS are super-safe Treasury bonds issued for 10, 20 or 30 years which pay you a percentage of their face value, adjusted by the consumer price index twice a year, as described in Chapter 2.

You can protect yourself against unanticipated inflation by holding TIPS directly or by buying a variable annuity which uses a mutual fund of TIPS. We have already covered the downsides of variable annuities including fees which can be high and the fact that, unlike Single Payment Immediate Annuities (SPIAs), variable annuities don't protect you against getting stupid and vulnerable and being "convinced" to pull out your money. Variable annuities also don't give you a fixed amount of income every month since the returns on TIPS mutual funds vary with the fluctuating rates paid by the bonds purchased regularly by the funds.

When you own shares in a TIPS mutual fund you don't own the actual bonds: rather you own a share of all the TIPS held by the fund. TIPS fund managers stay busy buying new bonds to accommodate an influx of new mutual fund money and occasionally selling bonds to pay for customer withdrawals and to replace older bonds that have matured. Therefore, the average maturity of the bonds in the fund and the rates that they pay will also keep changing. This is not under your control as it would be if you owned the TIPS directly and returns from TIPS mutual funds are therefore somewhat less predictable than returns from TIPS owned directly.

In recent years, as rates have fallen on all types of government bonds and the fear of possible inflation has increased, TIPS have become very popular, which means that the government can sell them at very low (sometimes negative) inflation-adjusted rates. These low rates, combined with the often high variable annuity fees and a portfolio of TIPS bonds which can vary in maturity, has decreased the returns on variable annuities backed by TIPS to almost nothing. Yes, you still get protection against inflation, but the cost is the lack of a meaningful positive rate of return. Toward mid-year 2013, rates on all types of bonds, including TIPS increased when the Federal Reserve announced their intention to stop quantitative easing which would allow interest rates to go up as the economy improved.

It is generally better to hold TIPS yourself, rather than through a mutual fund or variable annuity. This is true for two reasons. If you hold TIPS yourself it is less expensive because you don't have to pay an annual management fee to a mutual fund, an insurance company or both. Annual fees on mutual funds made of TIPS generally range from a quarter of a percent to as high as a full percent or more. Also, if you buy TIPS yourself, you can get a pure portfolio that meets your needs. If you buy only 30 year TIPS that pay, say, 2 percent interest, adjusted for inflation, you will get that real rate of return until the bonds mature.[56] If you buy TIPS in the form of a mutual fund or variable annuity, you will get a blend of bonds with maturities ranging from a year or less up to 30 years and that uncertain blend will pay far less than 30 year TIPS.

There are many ways to buy TIPS. Your broker can buy them for you but a commission will be charged. Your bank can also buy them for you but they will charge you a fee for the service. You can save the commission and all fees by buying them on your own through TreasuryDirect, on online service of the Treasury. This will be covered in greater detail in Chapter 5 of this book.

An advantage of owning TIPS through TreasuryDirect, aside from the inflation protection, is that the semi-annual interest, as well as the face value of any bonds that mature, are paid directly to your bank account, electronically. Since you can buy TIPS with maturities up to 30 years, this will guarantee lifetime income that will keep up with inflation, without paying fees to anyone. If you want to structure the payout of your principal as well, you can buy bonds with other than 10, 20 or 30 year maturities (such as 12 year, 14 year, 16 year, etc.) through TreasuryDirect's secondary market and as the bonds mature, more funds will flow into your account.

A disadvantage of buying TIPS yourself is that they are a bond rather than an annuity. This means that they do not provide insurance against living too long. In Chapter 5 we will show how to use TIPS to provide inflation protection for a fixed annual payment that you might have in the form of defined benefit pension payments which lack COLAs. However, a fairly large investment in TIPS is currently needed to inflation-protect a much smaller amount of annual income. In a similar manner, you may choose to purchase a fixed immediate annuity to close your lifetime income gap and then protect yourself against much of the damage that could be done by inflation by also purchasing TIPS. If you get a quote on an annuity with and without inflation protection, you may want to compare it to the cost of the pension protection you could get on your own by buying TIPS.

Joint Annuities

If you are married or in a committed relationship, you may want to provide annuity income for your spouse or partner. A simple way of doing this is to purchase an annuity for each partner. Another possibility is to purchase a joint annuity, which provides survivorship income for the surviving spouse.

Suppose that Joe (the "primary annuitant') is purchasing a life annuity for his own life but wishes to protect his wife, Irene (the "joint annuitant"), in the event that he dies before her. The cost of that annuity to the insurance company depends on three things: Joe's age, Irene's age, and the proportion of Joe's annuity that he wishes to have Irene receive after his death. It is important to note that the higher this proportion, (and the younger his wife) the greater the expected payout the insurance company expects to make and the higher the lump sum cost of the annuity.

The basic method of estimating the life expectancy of a joint annuitant is to take the life expectancy of the primary annuitant (in this case, Joe) and add to that the life expectancy of the survivor (Irene) at the expected age of the primary annuitant's death. In the case of Joe and Irene (if Irene were to get 100 percent of Joe's annuity at his death) you would add to Joe's life expectancy the life expectancy of Irene at the expected age of Joe's death. If Joe is 2 years older than Irene and wishes to retire at age 65, he would have a life expectancy of 18 years (on the Social Security tables) and would be expected to die at age 83. Irene at age 81 (her age at the time of Joe's expected death) would have a life expectancy of nearly 9 years. Therefore the insurance company would expect to pay out the annuity for 18 plus 9 or 27 years.

If Irene is to receive only half of Joe's annuity, the 9 years she is expected to live at Joe's death are divided by 2 giving an equivalent payment of 4.5 years and a total life expectancy of 18 plus 4.5 or 22.5 years. This is essentially how the cost (or payout) of a joint annuity is calculated, ignoring insurance company fees and the fact that they may use a different life expectancy table.

Estimating the Survivorship Percent

When a married person buys an annuity, he or she must choose the percentage of the annuity that will go to the survivor. The higher the percentage, the lower the amount of the annual payment made when both parties are alive. Therefore, for a given lump sum investment in an annuity, the more the annuity buyer receives, the less the survivor will receive.

The pension laws in the US guarantee a spouse a minimum of 50 percent survivorship benefits from (work-related) pension annuities unless the spouse signs away that right. Note that this does not apply to annuities purchased with after-tax dollars, only those purchased with pension money in a 401(k), an IRA, a Keogh, etc. Fifty percent seems like a reasonable starting point since the surviving spouse will need at least half the income of the married couple. However, closer inspection reveals that many of the expenses of retired couples are fixed expenses that will not diminish at the death of one.

Two of the largest expenses are housing and transportation (auto). Housing costs are likely to remain the same after the death of one spouse unless the other spouse deliberately moves and downsizes housing.

Furthermore, to the extent that one party contributed substantially to home production (cooking, cleaning, gardening, repairs) the surviving spouse may have to pay more to replace those services. Certainly food, clothing and health care costs will be diminished with the death of a spouse, but the total savings to the household will often be less than a quarter. A quick estimate can be made by estimating the proportion of total expenses that are fixed and splitting the non-fixed costs. For example, if housing, automobile and gifts to family total half of all expenses, the savings from the death of a spouse will be only half of the variable half or a quarter. This implies a 75 percent survivorship amount is necessary.

Nest Eggs and Estates

Two important factors have been omitted from the calculation of the lump sum needed at retirement. These are the desire on the part of many people to maintain a certain fixed sum of money as a "nest egg" against which they will not draw and the somewhat related concept of leaving a fixed sum of money to one's beneficiaries, be they relatives or charities.

The desire for a nest egg is often based on the need for liquidity. In retirement, people often have a high need for liquidity based largely upon expected health difficulties and the need to advance cash for certain treatments. By placing *all* your assets in an immediate annuity, you give up your liquidity, forcing yourself to live from annuity check to annuity check. It is generally a good idea to keep 3 to 6 months' worth of expenses in liquid form, particularly if expensive emergencies related to health, home repair or other events are commonplace in your life.

Since an immediate annuity converts your assets into a series of payments guaranteed for life, the more of your assets you put into an annuity, the less will be available for your estate. This may create a tension between your desire to maintain your standard of living for the remainder of your life, no matter how long that will be, and your desire to leave a legacy to your heirs (or to a charity). As mentioned elsewhere in this book, this tension probably accounts for some of the lack of popularity of annuities. The easiest solution is to designate the amount of your assets that will be left to your estate. For many people, this will be larger if there are heirs with special needs. Much of the remaining assets can then be annuitized to create additional income for life.

Annuities with Guarantees

While the purpose of buying a life annuity is to sustain core expenses for the rest of your life, some potential buyers hesitate to make the upfront investment because they worry about dying soon thereafter without getting much back. Therefore, virtually all immediate annuities offer you the opportunity (at a cost) to guarantee that if you die, your heirs will receive the payments that would have gone to you for a certain number of years. Typical guarantee products offer a 5 to 20 year "period certain" feature in which your payment will be made to you or to you estate for at least that number of years. For example, if you buy a life annuity with a 5-year period-certain option and die after a year, your monthly payments will be made to your estate for the remaining 4 years.

The cost of the guarantee is built into the reduced lifetime payment that you will receive. The table below gives an example of the size of the reduction for the period certain feature ranging from 5 to 20 years for a 70 year old man and a 70 year old woman living in the State of Washington.

With no period certain guarantees, a 70 year-old man would get a lifetime cash flow of 7.92 percent of his investment while a 70 year-old woman would get a cash-flow of 7.08 percent. The cost of a 5-year period certain guarantee would be a 1.89 percent *decrease* in the annual payment for the man and 1.13 percent for the woman. The low cost is partly due to the low probability that they will die so soon and partly due to the fact that the company has to make a maximum of 5 payments which are likely to occur in the future. At the other extreme, the cost of a 20 year guarantee is 22.34 percent decrease in payments for the man and 14.35 percent for the woman.

Table 4
Cash-Flow from an Immediate Annuity and the Cost of Period Certain Guarantees for 70 Year Olds in the State of Washington

Guarantee	Male Cash Flow	Cost Male Guarantee	Female Cash Flow	Cost Female Guarantee
None	7.92%		7.08%	
5 Year	7.77%	1.89%	7.00%	1.13%
10 Year	7.46%	5.92%	6.86%	3.14%
15 Year	6.85%	14.34%	6.27%	11.81%
20 Year	6.39%	22.34%	6.18%	14.35%

Buying Annuities When Rates are Low

If you decide to buy an annuity, should you put all your money in now or should you wait until today's super-low interest rates start moving back up? An alternative is to *time diversify* (sometimes called "laddering" or "dollar cost averaging") by purchasing several annuities over a few years, giving yourself the opportunity to capture at least some of the increase in interest rates, if it does occur.

To see whether it is worth waiting until interest rates go back up, it is useful to look again at Table 1, shown earlier in this chapter to see how much your annuity payment would increase if rates went up. As you can see, a 50 percent increase in interest rates (internal rates of return) from 2 percent (close to the current level) to 3 percent would increase annual payments on a $200,000 immediate fixed annuity for a man age 70 from $16,802 to $17,986, an increase of just 7 percent in the annual payment. For a woman aged 70 it would be an increase of 8 percent because women have greater life expectancies than men of the same age and will earn interest longer.

The younger you are, the greater the difference would be because the money is expected to be paid out over a longer time and will earn more interest. For a man of 60, an increase in interest rates from 2 to 3 percent adds 10.3 percent and for a woman of 60, it adds 11.7 percent.

Remember that these increases only apply if you get the higher rate on the day you fund your annuity, not if rates go up gradually over time. And it also ignores the return that you can be getting on your money as you wait to fully fund the annuity (the "opportunity cost" of the money). If the annuity has an internal rate of return of 2 percent and you can get 2 percent on your own, you break even by time diversifying your money into the annuity over 2 or more years (although you do lose the ability to tax defer the interest that you earn for those years, which is a pretty small savings).

In conclusion, if you truly believe that interest rates are likely to increase substantially over the next few years, and you are right, you can gain a small amount of additional payment by splitting your money into two or three parts and buying an annuity each year. Unless interest rates go up by a large proportion in the near future, the size and probability of the additional payment may be too small to justify putting off the purchase of the annuity, particularly if you worry that you might not ever follow through on your multi-year purchase plan. Don't forget, you aren't getting any smarter!

On the other hand, there doesn't appear to be much payout benefit to buying a larger annuity at one time than several smaller annuities spaced over time. Payouts are largely proportional to the money invested.

Free Look Period

For many seniors, the purchase of an annuity represents the commitment of a large portion of their valuable assets. When you combine this risk with the large rewards given to those who sell high-commission annuities (generally variable annuities), it is not surprising that most states have regulations that allow those who have actually purchased an annuity to get their money back if they change their minds within a specified period of time. This time can vary substantially by state but is most often at least 10 days. In fact, to reduce elder fraud, many states give senior citizens (often those over 65) additional time to reconsider their annuity purchase.

The period during which an annuity buyer can change his or her mind is called a "free look" or "right to return" period. If state law permits a free look period, it generally insists that this feature is prominently explained in the annuity contract.

We once had an elderly friend who had more than enough pension and Social Security income to live a comfortable life until she died. She also had a large portfolio of investments designated in her will to go to her favorite charities. One night she called in shame and panic and admitted that a fast-talking salesperson convinced her to put nearly all her assets into a variable annuity that would be expensive and do her no good. Using the free look period law, we were fortunately able to get her out of this contract.

Risk of the Annuity

Since a fixed annuity promises a set monthly payment for life, what are the chances that the company that offers it will go out of business, cutting off your payments? In general, the probability that your insurance company will stop making payments on your annuity are very small, largely because states regulate insurance companies in a very conservative manner, forcing them to hold large reserves to protect policy holders.

However, insurance companies do occasionally fail. For example, in 1991 Executive Life Insurance Company, the largest insurance company in California and a major issuer of annuities, failed. While most of their obligations were taken over by another insurance company, payouts were missed or cut for many months, and even today it does not appear that all policy holders will be repaid in full. More recently, The Hartford, one of the nation's oldest and largest issuers of annuities, had to be rescued from failure by an injection of $3.4 billion by the US Government's TARP program in 2009. In April 2012, it announced that it was getting out of the annuity business.

It must be noted that the failure of an insurance company has the greatest effect on owners of immediate annuities. This is because the owner of the annuity has paid in all of his or her money in exchange for a lifetime of future payments. In contrast, someone who has a property/liability policy or even a term life insurance policy with a company that fails can just find a new insurer and start paying premiums to them.

Since we know that issuers of annuities can fail (although failure is very rare) and the consequences of such failure can be great, what happens to you if you own one of their annuities? A principal source of compensation for those who have annuities with failed insurance companies is the assets of the company that issued the annuity. Insurance companies hold a lot of assets whose liquidity ranges from cash to stocks and bonds to real estate. It can take a year or more for the assets to be liquidated and paid out to annuity holders, which means that annuity payments may be missed or cut, and in many cases, these assets may not be sufficient to pay all obligations which means that annuity holders may not be repaid in full by their companies. However, state insurance funds may help make up the difference.

State Insurance Funds

Unlike most large banks which are regulated by large, sophisticated federal bank regulators, insurance companies are regulated by states and not by the federal government. Most large, national insurance companies are licensed to do business in every state. To insure consumers against failure of their insurance company, states generally require those doing business in a state to participate in a state guaranty fund or guaranty association. Insurance companies pay a fee based upon the size of its business into a fund maintained to help pay off the obligations of insurance companies that fail.

If you own an annuity, your coverage depends on the state in which the policy was issued. Table 4 shows the maximum amount that can be paid out to cover the present value of an annuity. As you can see, the most common size of the maximum annuity payout is $100,000 and the largest is $500,000. This implies that if you want to buy an immediate annuity costing more than the state insurance fund maximum payment, you could increase your safety, at little additional cost, by diversifying or splitting your purchase between 2 or more companies.

In the event that an insurance company fails, the state insurance commissioner generally takes control of its assets and tries to find another insurance company to take over its business. If there is a shortfall, the guarantee fund would typically try to cover it. If the reserves of the guarantee fund are insufficient, states are generally allowed to charge other insurance companies registered in the state up to 2 percent of the "net direct written premiums" to raise additional funds and replenish reserves.[57]

Table 5
Maximum Payout to Cover the present Value of an Annuity by State

State	Insurance	State	Insurance
Alabama	$100,000	Missouri	$100,000
Alaska	$100,000	Montana	$250,000
Arizona	$100,000	Nebraska	$100,000
Arkansas	$300,000	Nevada	$100,000
California	80% not to exceed $250,000	New Hampshire	$100,000
Colorado	$250,000	New Jersey	$100,000
Connecticut	$500,000	New Mexico	$100,000
Delaware	$250,000	New York	$500,000
Dist. of Col	$300,000	No. Carolina	$300,000
Florida	$250,000	North Dakota	$100,000
Georgia	$100,000	Ohio	$250,000
Hawaii	$100,000	Oklahoma	$300,000
Idaho	$250,000	Oregon	$250,000
Illinois	$250,000	Pennsylvania	$100,000
Indiana	$100,000	Puerto Rico	$100,000
Iowa	$250,000	Rhode Island	$250,000
Kansas	$250,000	So. Carolina	$300,000
Kentucky	$250,000	South Dakota	$100,000
Louisiana	$250,000	Tennessee	$250,000
Maine	$250,000	Texas	$250,000
Maryland	$250,000	Utah	$200,000
Massachusetts	$100,000	Vermont	$250,000
Michigan	$250,000	Virginia	$250,000
Minnesota	$250,000	Washington	$500,000
Mississippi	$100,000	West Virginia	$250,000
		Wisconsin	$300,000
		Wyoming	$100,000

Source: AnnuityAdvantage.com June 24, 2012

Insurance Company Ratings

When you decide to buy an annuity, you will probably want to buy from one or more companies that are in the best financial condition to minimize the (small) risk that they can fail. A number of rating agencies rate companies that offer annuities. AM Best specializes in the insurance industry and its ratings are very highly regarded. Moody's and Standard & Poor's also rate insurance companies along with companies in other industries.

In general, you want to buy from a highly-rated company because they will tend to have the greatest financial strength. The highest Best rating is A++ followed by A+ and A. It is not generally advisable to buy an annuity from a company rated below A.

Perhaps the easiest way to find out a company's ratings is to Google "Best rating "Company Name." For example, when I entered "Best rating USAA" in June of 2012, the following appeared.

Table 6
Ratings of USAA

Agency	Rating
A.M. Best Company	**A++** A plus plus (Superior, highest of 16 possible ratings)
Moody's Investors Service	**Aa1** Double A one (Excellent, second highest of 21 possible ratings)
Standard & Poor's	**AA+** Double A plus (Very Strong, second highest of 21 possible ratings)
Ward's 50	USAA Life Insurance companies were named to Ward's 50 for the 18th year. Ward's 50 is a benchmarking group of top-performing insurance companies. (2011)

Table 7
AM Best Financial Strength Ratings of Life and
Annuity Companies Over $2 Billion (June 24, 2002)

Company	Rating	Company	Rating
AGC Life Insurance Company	A	Midland National	A+
AXA Equitable Life Insurance	A	Minnesota Life	A+
Aetna Life Insurance Company	A+	Monumental Life	A+
Allianz Life Insurance Co of NA	A	Munich American	A+
Allstate Life Insurance Company	A	Nationwide	A+
American Family Lf Assur Co	A+	New England Life	A+
American General Assurance	A+	New York Life	A++
American General Life	A	North American Company	A+
American Heritage Life	A	Northwestern Mutual Life	A++
American National	A+	Pacific Life	A+
Aviva Life and Annuity	A	Parker Centennial	A+
Berkshire Hathaway	A	Paul Revere	B++
Brooke Life Insurance Company	A++	Principal Life	A+
C M Life Insurance Company	A+	Protective Life	A+
Cigna Life Insurance Company	A++	Provident Life	A
Colonial Life & Accident	A	Pruco Life	A+
Companion Life Insurance	A	Prudential	A+
Connecticut General	A+	ReliaStar	A
First Great-West Life & Annuity	A	RiverSource	A+
First MetLife Investors	A+	SCOR Global	A
First Penn-Pacific Life	A+	Securian	A+
First Symetra National Life	A+	Security Life	A
First Unum Life Insurance	A	Southern Farm Bureau Life	A+
General American Life	A	State Farm	A++
General Re Life Corporation	A+	Stonebridge	A+
Genworth Life and Annuity	A++	Sun Life and Health	A+
Great-West Life & Annuity	A	SunAmerica	A
Guardian Insurance & Annuity	A+	Swiss Re	A+
Hannover Life Reassurance	A++	Symetra	A
Hartford	A	TIAA-CREF	A++
ING	A	Thrivent	A++
Jackson National	A	Transamerica	A+
John Hancock	A+	Unimerica	A
Lafayette Life	A+	United States Life	A
Life Insurance Company of North America	A+	United World	A+
Lincoln Life & Annuity	A	United of Omaha	A+
MML Bay State Life	A+	Unum	A
MONY	A++	Variable Annuity	A
Massachusetts Mutual	A+	West Coast Life	A+
Metropolitan Life Insurance	A++	Western National	A
Metropolitan Tower Life	A+	Western Reserve Life	A+
	A+	Western and Southern Life	A+

Companies with high ratings will be proud of them and will display their current rankings. You can also find out Best ratings by going to their web site "AMBest.com" and signing up (for free) to get access to their most current ratings of life and annuity companies. When I asked for the ratings of companies with at least $2 billion in policies, I came up with the list in Table 7 on June 24, 2012[58]. Since ratings change all the time, this table should be used for purposes of illustration only.

Reverse Mortgage Annuities

A lot of retirees find that their income during retirement is less than that needed to maintain their standard of living. Many of these also lack the financial assets to boost their lifetime income with the purchase of an annuity.

Fortunately, many of the folks who fall into this category are homeowners who can convert the equity in their homes into additional lifetime income through a *reverse mortgage*. Instead of making monthly mortgage payments to the lender, as most homeowners did when they were younger, the reverse mortgage reverses the process and allows them to *receive* a monthly payment for the rest of their lives. Homeowners do this, in essence, by taking out a special kind of mortgage that doesn't have to be repaid until they die and their house is sold. In other words, a reverse mortgage allows homeowners to age in place in their home for as long as they live *and* to receive a monthly annuity check for the rest of their lives, if they like. Some deal!

While reverse mortgages can be a very valuable tool for older homeowners, these homeowners have to be very careful when they choose a company that offers reverse mortgages. Just one reverse mortgage plan is approved and insured by the U.S. Federal Government. This is called a *Home Equity Conversion Mortgage* or *HECM*, and is only available through an FHA (Federal Housing Authority) approved lender. You can find a list of these government-approved reverse mortgage lenders in your area on the Government's web site http://portal.hud.gov/hudportal/HUD?src=/program_offices /housing/sfh/hecm/hecmhome

There are also private reverse mortgage lenders who are unapproved by and unaffiliated with the US government. You may see their ads on late-night TV with pitchmen whom you might recognize as minor celebrity has-beens. Many of these private lenders seek to separate older Americans from their last remaining asset so be careful when you evaluate reverse mortgages. The maximum HECM loan is $650,000 (while private reverse mortgages have no limit) and it is available to people over age 62. You do need to pay a fee of $125 for a qualified housing counselor who will review it with you.

If you decide to take out a government-approved and insured reverse mortgage, title to your home remains with you. However, the reverse mortgage, like all home mortgages, places a lien on the property which gives the lender the right to sell your home when you (and your spouse, if you have one) die or move from the home. According to the Consumer Financial Protection Bureau "All reverse mortgage loans become due and payable when the last surviving borrower permanently moves out of the home. Typically, a 'permanent move' means that neither you nor any other co-borrower has lived in your home for one continuous year."[59]

At the death of the last spouse or when he or she permanently moves out of the house, any remaining equity after the lender is repaid will go to the estate. If, however, the home cannot be sold for at least the amount that is owed on it, the *lender* is out of luck. For that reason, reverse mortgage lenders will be very conservative when deciding how much of your equity they will give you. The fraction of the equity that you can take out of your home in a reverse mortgage (as a lump sum or in the form of an annuity) is known as the Principal Limit Factor (PLF).

The money given to you is treated as a loan (that you don't have to repay) but interest compounds on the loan each month and keeps growing and offsetting your remaining equity. The older you are when you take out the reverse mortgage, the greater will be the percentage of your home equity advanced to you since your life expectancy will be shorter.

There are upfront fees and monthly fees for the standard FHA loan. Fees are generally higher, often much higher, for private reverse mortgages.

The money taken from home equity in a reverse mortgage can be used for anything, and may be a useful way to pay off a mortgage. In fact, repayment of any outstanding mortgage is generally a requirement of a reverse mortgage. The remaining proceeds from a reverse mortgage can be generally taken as a lump sum, an annuity for as long as you live in your home (called a "tenure annuity") or for a shorter period of your choice, or as a line of credit, or some combination of the three. As shown below, if you are interested in using a reverse mortgage to generate lifetime income, it may be to your advantage to take a lump sum and use it to buy a Single Payment Immediate Annuity from a reputable insurance company offering the highest monthly payment for that lump sum. You are not obligated to take the tenure annuity offered by the reverse mortgage lender.

You cannot get out all of the equity in your home through a reverse mortgage. The percentage of the assessed value of your equity that you can borrow depends on your age and the rate of interest that is being charged. The younger you are when you apply for a reverse mortgage, the smaller the percentage of your home value that you can get. Similarly, the higher the interest rate at the time of your application, the smaller the percentage you can get. The reasoning behind this is that the lender (or the insurer for the lender) wants to sell the house when the owners have died for more than the amount owed on it in order to at least break even. The younger the borrowers, the longer they are expected to live and the greater the balance will grow at interest. Similarly, the higher the interest rate, the greater will be owed by the homeowners at their death.

Table 8 below tells you approximately what percentage of your home equity (the assessed value of the home minus any money you owe on it) you can access through a reverse mortgage, at the beginning of 2013. At an interest rate of 5 percent, a 62 year old could borrow up to 61.9 percent of the equity in his or her home while a 72 year old could borrow up to 67.7 percent. Remember that the maximum loan from an FHA mortgage is currently $650,000 so a 72 year old could get that amount only if the equity in the house was worth $960,118.[60]

HECM Saver Reverse Mortgage
A major expense of the standard reverse mortgage is the cost of the insurance premium needed to protect the lender in case it cannot get its money out when the borrower dies. This will happen if the borrower lives so long that the amount borrowed plus accumulated interest is greater than the value of the home when they die. It could also happen if the house loses value over this period

Table 8
Home Equity Conversion Mortgage (HECM) Standard
Principal Limit Factors (PLFs)

	Expected Interest Rate				
Age	**4.5%**	**5.0%**	**5.5%**	**6.0%**	**6.50%**
62	.619	.619	.548	.494	.447
72	.677	.677	.616	.568	.527
82	.730	.730	.680	.641	.605
92	.776	.776	.740	.708	.681

Neighborhood Reinvestment Corporation **Introduction to Home Equity Conversion Mortgages, 2012 p44**

When you apply for a standard HECM reverse mortgage, your insurance fee is 2 percent of the amount borrowed, upfront, and 1.25 percent of the amount borrowed per year. If you borrow $500,000, for example, the upfront insurance cost would be $10,000 and the annual insurance fee would be $6,250.

There is a second type of FHA reverse mortgage known as a "Saver" reverse mortgage. The main difference between a saver and a standard reverse mortgage is that the "saver" eliminates most of the 2 percent up-front insurance fee in exchange for reducing the percentage of the value of your home you can borrow. Table 6 shows the Principal Limit Factors for the HECM Saver. To use our familiar example, with a 5 percent interest rate a 72 year old could borrow only 54.4 percent of the value of the home with the *saver* reverse mortgage as opposed to 67.7 percent with a *standard* reverse mortgage (as you saw in Table 5). To get the maximum $650,000 loan with a saver reverse mortgage, the house would have to be worth $1,195,853.[61]

Table 9
HECM Saver Principal Limit Factors

	Expected Interest Rate				
Age	4.50%	5.00%	5.50%	6.00%	6.50%
62	.523	.523	.456	.399	.347
72	.544	.544	.498	.449	.398
82	.583	.583	.538	.50	.460
92	.610	.610	.576	.542	.511

Neighborhood Reinvestment Corporation **Introduction to Home Equity Conversion Mortgages,** 2012http://www.hecmcounselors.org/sites/default/files/uploads/HO111%20Manual_Chris_LBedits07162012.pdf p45

Buy Your Own Annuity

If your primary purpose in considering a reverse mortgage is to increase your lifetime income, you are generally better off taking a lump sum from your reverse mortgage and buying a single payment immediate annuity yourself rather than taking the "tenure" annuity option from the HECM program. Professor Jack Guttentag[62] looked at both options in December, 2009 for an 86 year old male whose house was worth $400,000 and whose borrowing limit was $288,000. While this amount would provide an annuity of $2,444 per month within the HECM program for as long as he lived in the house (called a "tenure annuity"), if he drew the $288,000 in cash, he could use it to purchase a monthly annuity of $3,778 from a life insurance company. He would do 55 percent better by using the proceeds from the reverse mortgage to buy his own annuity.

Of course, we are not comparing apples to apples here. With a single payment immediate annuity (without survivorship benefits) purchased from an insurance company, heirs inherit nothing from the annuity when the annuity purchaser dies, even if death occurs soon after purchase. With a tenure annuity from HECM, the purchaser can convert the remaining value of his annuity to a line of credit at any time. The younger the tenure annuity holder at the time of conversion, the greater will be the line of credit. If the conversion is done when he or she becomes seriously ill, the amount remaining in the line of credit can be passed onto that person's heirs[63]. The flexibility and liquidity provided to those who choose the tenure annuity is costly to the lender which results in substantially lower annuity payments than those paid by regular Single Payment Immediate Annuities available from many insurance companies.

Another downside to the tenure annuity, aside from its lower payment, is the fact that it is paid only as long as the owner continues to live in the home. If he moves to a nursing home, for example, the annuity payments stop.

Professor Guttentag does caution those thinking about using a reverse mortgage to fund an annuity to shop for both, separately, rather than taking a "deal" from a company that packages them together since it "obscures the pricing of both." He goes on to say; "If a loan provider or an insurance agent talks to you about drawing funds from a HECM to purchase an annuity, run like a thief. He is looking to make two commissions from you, and they both are likely to be extortionate." He concludes by saying: "Doing it yourself means that you avoid being solicited. Seniors who are taken advantage of are almost always seniors who have been solicited by fast-talking scamsters. You refuse to be exploited by refusing to be solicited."

A disadvantage of taking Professor Guttentag's advice is that the average age of those taking on a reverse mortgage is well into the 70s when the ability to shop for two complex products may be diminished. Therefore, if you know that you need additional lifetime income and you have a home with considerable equity, you may want to get an FHA reverse mortgage sooner, rather than later, and use at least some of the proceeds to fund an annuity.

It is important to note that the FHA has been losing money on the reverse mortgages that it insures, partly because some borrowers have been unable to keep up with their property taxes. As a result, some changes have been made to save money for the program in the future. One such change, which went into effect April 1, 2013, was the elimination of the fixed rate option on lump sum payments. A second change, proposed for October 1, 2013, is a closer look at the credit rating and overall financial ability of applicants to handle their loans. While reverse mortgages will still be around in the future, they may become more expensive and more difficult to get.

Conclusions

Annuities are great for providing lifetime income that is safe from both market fluctuations and mistakes that we might otherwise make as we age. Essentially they can protect us against three important risks: *longevity risk* or the risk of living longer than our life expectancy, *market risk* or the risk that our income will fall if stock prices or interest rates go down, and what we might call *judgment (or "stupidity") risk* which is the risk that we might do something to harm the lifetime income stream on which we depend.

An annuity works because it collects an upfront payment from a large number of people who seek income for life. The size of this payment is based on the annual payment desired and the person's life expectancy. For every person who lives longer than his or her life expectancy and collects extra payments, someone lives shorter than life expectancy and gives up those payments.

In this book our focus is on guaranteeing sufficient income for life. As a result, we pay special attention to the Single Payment Immediate Annuity (SPIA). This type of annuity, which is sold by most life insurance companies, can provide fixed monthly payments for life. Since payments are fixed, they eliminate market risk. Since they pay for life, they eliminate longevity risk. And since they can't be cashed in, they eliminate judgment or *stupidity* risk. A few companies will sell them with inflation protection as well (at an extra cost).

For those seeking to supplement their lifetime income, Single Payment Immediate Annuities offer the huge benefit of generating much more guaranteed income than any other type of investment. While a 70 year old man could get a safe return of perhaps 2 1/2 percent by investing in long-term US Treasury bonds, he could get a guaranteed cash flow of nearly 8 percent for life by investing in an annuity. The higher payment results from two factors: part of it is return of your own principal that you invested and part is due to the fact that it is an annuity where those who die early (before their life expectancy) pay for those who live longer.

A possible downside of an immediate annuity is that if you die soon after putting in your money, your estate gets nothing back from your investment. However, if your primary concern is protecting your own standard of living for life, this may not be an issue. It is possible to guarantee lifetime income from your annuity for a second person, perhaps a spouse, and it is also possible to guarantee payments for a minimum number of years, such as 5 or 10, if you die early. These added guarantees come at extra cost which translates into a lower annuity payment for life.

In spite of their benefits and the near-universal endorsement by economists, life annuities are not very popular with consumers. Why more people don't take advantage of this remarkable product is called by economists the "annuity puzzle." This is likely due to the fact that annuities have not been marketed very well to consumers who value present consumption far more than consumption in an indefinite future.

Some people are reluctant to buy an immediate annuity because market interest rates are currently very low. This is an argument you may hear from your broker or financial advisor who earns a fee for money that they manage for you. While this concern may be valid for the purchase of other fixed income products, such as bonds, it is far less important for immediate annuities since most of the guaranteed monthly cash flow is due to return of your own investment, not to earnings on the investment.

If you have sufficient income to meet your core expenses for many years, but not quite enough to provide for unexpected longevity, you can purchase a fixed deferred annuity. In return for a payment now, you will be guaranteed payments for life beginning at a future age that you get to choose. Therefore, if you are 70 now, you might choose to purchase a deferred annuity that will pay you $5,000 per month for life beginning when you turn 85. The cost of a deferred annuity which pays you $5,000 every month is much less than the cost of an immediate annuity that pays the same $5,000 per month.

Life insurance companies that issue annuities are highly regulated by the states in which the policies are issued and are generally considered to be safe. To be even safer, it is useful to buy policies from companies that have the highest financial strength ratings. To make annuities less risky to buyers, states have insurance funds that will reimburse annuity holders in the unlikely event that an insurance company fails.

Homeowners without the financial assets needed to buy an annuity may consider a reverse mortgage. These will allow you to live in your current home for the rest of your life and also receive guaranteed lifetime monthly income through an annuity funded directly or indirectly by this mortgage. Reverse mortgages approved by the US Government and insured by the FHA are called HECM (Home Equity Credit Mortgages). These are, by far, the safest reverse mortgages on the market.

Chapter 4
Someone to Watch Over Me?

At a Glance

Every few days, it seems, those of us who are older and have accumulated a few bucks seem to get invitations to a luncheon or dinner to learn how we can do *really well* in our retirement. Lots of people want to help us manage our money. Some of these financial advisors are really good and some are even reasonably priced. Far too few are both, forcing us to choose between spending a large part of our often meager returns on good advisors, a smaller amount on mediocre, poor or even dishonest advisors or trying to figure out a lot of this ourselves.

This chapter will look at the ways we can turn over some or all of our financial decision-making to others and the qualifications they should have to give us good advice and wisely handle our money. It also examines how financial advisors are compensated for helping to manage our money and the extent to which their incentives are aligned with our interests.

Nearly three-quarters of US retail investors seek advice from a financial adviser before purchasing shares of stock. There are three basic ways in which you can pay for the services of your financial advisor: by the hour, through a commission based on the products that you buy or as a percentage of the assets that the advisor manages for you.

While there are many legitimate services that a financial advisor can provide for you, far too many advisors sell themselves by making the false claim that they can help you *beat* the market. This is a fallacy -- nobody beats the market over many years without taking on higher than average risk unless they are lucky, so it is not worth trying. You can do as well as the market, however, through buying and holding stock indexes that are both inexpensive and widely available. You can even do this easily yourself, saving the fees that you would otherwise pay to a financial advisor.

A possible problem of working with a stockbroker, financial planner or financial advisor is that your interests may not be aligned. The need for financial professionals to earn money may cause them to sell you products that you don't need, turn over your stocks more than necessary to generate trading commissions, or discourage you from purchasing a useful annuity because it lowers the amount of money they manage for you and this reduces the fees charged for that management.

To what extent will financial advisors truly watch over you, preventing you from making age-related errors in judgment? In many cases, privacy laws keep them from revealing your increasingly erratic actions to anyone, including your children, unless you sign a waiver well in advance of your deterioration.

Who Can Be Trusted?

Who can be trusted to make financial decisions for you when you are no longer capable of making them yourself? Should you trust a broker, a financial planner or an investment advisor? Or should you trust none of the above, setting your retirement financing largely on "automatic" while you still have the intelligence to do so?

This chapter examines the ways you can turn over some or all of your financial decision-making to others and the qualifications they should have to give you advice and handle your money. It also examines the ways in which they are compensated for helping to manage your money and whether their incentives are aligned with yours. How can you find someone who is honest, competent and fairly priced, and if you have actually found this holy grail, what happens if they age out of the profession before you age out of this world; in other words, how do you deal with succession when you are considerably older than you are now?

Qualifications

Most investors appear to rely on a financial advisor for investment decisions. A 2008 survey found that 73 percent of US retail investors seek advice from a financial adviser before purchasing shares.[64] This dependence on a financial advisor *increases* among investors who are better educated and more financially literate.[65]

Those who give financial advice may be stockbrokers, financial planners or investment advisors, some of whom work for banks as personal bankers or wealth managers. While there are different examinations and qualifications for each category, many of those who give financial advice are registered in two or more categories and the differences among the categories have become blurred and somewhat useless.

"Stockbrokers" are 'registered representatives' of a brokerage firm. They must pass a basic examination administered by the Financial Industry Regulatory Authority (FINRA), a self-regulatory organization that is overseen by the federal Securities and Exchange Commission (SEC). These days, most brokerage firms are also registered with the SEC or state governments as investment advisory firms and many (but not all) of their registered investment advisors have also passed the exam needed to be stockbrokers.

"While some investment advisers, financial planners and brokers may be credentialed as Certified Financial Planners (CFP®), no state or federal law requires these credentials." [66] It is not difficult to legally call yourself an investment advisor or financial planner. The only investment advisors who have to register with the SEC are those who manage $100 million or more in client assets. If they manage less, they need only register with their state. Only in recent years have *new* investment advisors had to pass a competency examination to register with their states. Older investment advisors may have been allowed to register without demonstrating their competence in any way.

There is some added protection that comes from using a financial advisor or planner who works for a brokerage firm. This protection arises from the fact that brokerage firms are much more tightly regulated and examined than investment advisors and financial planners who do not work for brokerage firms. According to a recent article by Senator Spencer Bachus:

"While average American investors may not fully understand the different titles that investment professionals use, they assume there is government oversight protecting their savings from fraud. And indeed, when you contract with a licensed broker-dealer to buy and sell stocks or commodities, there is a reasonable level of oversight, as broker-dealers face examinations of the accounts they manage on a regular and consistent basis.

"But the average investment adviser—who isn't registered as a broker and thus doesn't buy or sell stock—can expect to be examined only once a decade. Even worse, the Securities and Exchange Commission (SEC) reports that almost 40 percent of investment advisers have never been examined, or audited, meaning more Madoff-type Ponzi schemes could be afoot, and no one will know until investors are harmed."[67]

Certifications

There are many investment-related "certifications" that people can get, and it is often difficult to tell which are worthwhile since anyone can set up an organization to give out a new type of certification. Perhaps the most difficult and demanding certification relating to investments is the CFA – the Chartered Financial Analyst. This requires a college degree, work experience in the field and passing three very difficult examinations. Most CFAs specialize in evaluating the finances of *companies* in order to recommend that their employers or clients invest in them. However, about a quarter of the CFAs deal directly with consumers, particularly those with large amounts of money to invest. While CFAs may have demonstrated their ability to determine the value of companies (and they have proven through exams that they are smart and very knowledgeable about investments), their training and evaluation does not focus primarily on the financial needs of consumers.

Certified Public Accountants (CPAs) must also be college graduates (these days many states require 5 years of education rather than 4) and pass a demanding 5-part examination. Some CPAs specialize in individual taxes and may be in a position to talk with their clients about tax-related aspects of their investments. A reliable CPA may be a good source for a recommendation of an honest and competent planner, investment advisor or broker. However, only a small percentage of CPAs take much additional training in investments. Therefore, few CPAs are really qualified to give you much investment advice that doesn't have to do with taxes.

While new *Certified Financial Planners (CFPs)* need a college degree in any subject, those who became CFPs prior to 2007 did not need to be college graduates. The current coursework and examinations required for the CFP include the following:

General principles of financial planning
Insurance planning and risk management
Employee benefits planning
Investment planning
Income tax planning
Retirement planning
Estate planning

These days, many new CFPs are graduates of universities which offer the necessary courses as part of an accredited degree program. Since many of these programs are offered within business schools, graduates often have taken required background courses in accounting, finance, management, information processing, statistics and economics in addition to the CFP courses. In addition to earning a degree, they must also pass the special CFP examination. If you are thinking of using a CFP, find out if they have graduated from an accredited CFP program that is part of the business school of a well-respected university.

A *Masters of Business Administration (MBA)* degree from a good university generally indicates that an advisor has taken a rigorous course of study including accounting, finance and information technology, all of which are useful in advising others with their finances. A specialization in finance is particularly useful as are courses in investments, taxation, risk management (insurance) and real estate. However, many MBA programs offer no courses related to personal financial management and few offer more than one.

Experience and Street Smarts

Many, if not most of the best financial advisors I know, have none of the credentials mentioned above. What they have instead is a combination of experience, honesty and street smarts.

Jim

I was talking the other day to a high school classmate of mine who became a very successful financial advisor with a large, national brokerage firm in spite of never having earned a college degree. Let's call him "Jim."

When I asked Jim how someone should go about choosing a financial advisor, he said first, "Choose someone older, someone with lifetime experiences. Someone who is 60 is perfect! People need to have gone through kids and grandkids, aches and illnesses, healthcare expenses and financial crises in order to give sensible advice." He told me that his firm never even suggested that he get a financial planning credential although he does take courses offered by his firm in various products, most recently long-term health care and, when necessary, takes the examinations required by the regulators to sell these products.

And what about honesty? When a person has been in the business for 30 or 40 years and has worked for large firms with sophisticated compliance departments, a tendency toward dishonest, unfair or immoral treatment of customers is likely to have been discovered.

Jim suggests that the most important thing to know about financial advisors is how they manage their own money. In his experience, most financial advisors do a terrible job managing their own finances and cannot be trusted to manage someone else's. If he were shopping for someone to manage *his* money, he would ask to see *their* personal family accounts, although he expects that few would be willing to share this information with prospective clients. Does the financial advisor have the ability to manage his or her own money? Are they overleveraged on debt? Have they set up 529 plans to use government tax advantages to save for the education of their own children or grandchildren?

When Jim is interviewed by a potential client, he explains exactly how he does business. He tells them if their ideas are stupid and that he won't do something for them if he thinks it is wrong. He says that this degree of frankness and honesty is very difficult to find in a financial advisor. "Find someone who is so honest that he is in business for the fun of it. If someone needs your money, he may not be trustable."

Jim virtually never meets in person with his clients. If they have questions or concerns, he will talk to them on the phone, but even this is infrequent because he puts clients' money into long-term investments (generally mutual funds) compatible with their needs and doesn't believe that he can do better for them through additional management on his part.

118

This brings up the issue at the heart of this book. What happens when his older clients start "loosing" it? How can he spot it and what can he do about it?

Jim feels that he can recognize diminished cognitive capacity through telephone conversations. If a long-term client is having trouble remembering things and the questions he asks are totally different, he begins to suspect that they are "losing it." If they suddenly want to do something risky that is totally out of character, he first tries to reason with them and get them back on track, based on their long association. If he is unsuccessful and knows the client's children, he might have conversations with one or more child. Skirting the matter gently, so as not to violate his client's legal right to privacy, he will ask them if they've noticed anything unusual about mom or dad.

Paula

If Jim is a hands-off financial advisor who almost never sees his clients, Paula is just the opposite. Having just turned 60, Paula has been a broker and money manager for her entire career and started a small money management firm of her own 6 years ago after having run a large money management business for a bank.

Paula is a hands-on financial advisor in several ways. Not only does she make it a point to physically meet with her clients several times a year, she will buy and sell individual securities for them, as opposed to Jim who puts his clients into mutual funds that are managed by others. Paula's clients have given Paula the legal right to buy and sell securities on their behalf without seeking their permission in a "discretionary account" while Jim has no discretionary clients. In addition, Paula will even pay bills for her clients, if they wish, and tells her clients to call her whenever they have a problem. This has resulted, for example, in her having to sit with a sick client in a hospital room at 2:00 in the morning since the client had no one else to call.

Although Paula's business model is unlike Jim's, she meets all of Jim's criteria for an excellent financial advisor. She has had a lot of experience, she is scrupulously honest, she cares about her clients and she has her own financial house in good order.

Compensation of Financial Advisors

There are three basic ways in which you can pay for the services of your financial advisor:

• You can pay a fee by the hour, day, week, month or year

• You can pay a commission based on the products that you buy

• You can pay your financial advisor a percentage of the assets that he or she manages for you.

Some financial advisors use only one of these methods to charge their clients. Some use two or even all three. Jim, for example, receives all of his income in commissions. If he sells you mutual fund shares, he is compensated by the fund company which gives him a percentage of the sales, known as a "load." If he sells you insurance, he also gets a commission, some upfront and some on an ongoing basis if his client retains the policy.

Paula, on the other hand, earns most of her money from receiving a percentage of assets that she manages for her clients. She will also do some extra services for her clients for a fee, such as paying their bills. She doesn't handle insurance products directly, but will refer clients who need such products to associates whom she trusts to treat her clients efficiently and honestly.

Discretionary Power

Many consumers give discretionary power to their financial advisors to buy and sell investments on their behalf. The customer has the option of giving the financial advisor *limited trading authority* by signing a *limited trading authority* form or *full trading authority* by signing a *full trading authority form.* Limited trading authority authorizes the purchase or sale of investments for the account of a customer but does not permit the withdrawal of money or securities from the account. Full trading authority allows the withdrawal of money and securities from the account in addition to their purchase and sale. The legal instrument that authorizes limited trading authority is known as a "limited power of attorney." Full trading authority is authorized by a "full power of attorney."

Paula's clients give her limited trading authority so that she can buy or sell securities on their behalf. Jim does not require his clients to give him any trading authority at all.

Why would you want to sign over control of your investments to someone else? Some consumers feel that they are incapable of making decisions in an area in which they have limited knowledge. Others may be uninterested in finance and don't want to be bothered by routine questions from their advisor. Still others feel that the financial advisor may be far more knowledgeable than they are to guide their finances. A few consumers are convinced that their broker or financial advisor is smart enough to "beat" the market by more than any fee that they charge. Could they be right?

For several decades now, finance professors have examined whether investors are better off investing passively in a low-cost "index" of all stocks or paying an "expert" to beat the market through buying and selling in a clever manner. The results are clear and unambiguous – nobody beats the market, consistently and legally. Therefore, we can do as well as the market through buying and holding "the market" -- stock indexes that are both inexpensive and widely available. Why would we want to pay a "professional" a large part of our investment earnings for something that we can do for ourselves, virtually for free?

When I asked Jim about this, he offered the following analogy. "There are people out there who are great cooks and they can buy quality ingredients to prepare a wonderful meal, with wine, for less than 50 bucks. The rest of us have to spend $200 to take our wives out for a meal like this." In his experience, very few non-investment professionals feel that they know enough to manage their serious retirement money themselves, no matter how much they can save by doing so.

Even those of us who are "buy and hold" investors, who invest in a well-diversified portfolio of securities and forget about them, must make periodic decisions. Dividends and interest may pile up as cash in the account, earning virtually nothing until reinvested. Bonds may mature or be "called" if the bond issuer decides to pay them off early, turning earning assets into non-earning cash overnight. Some companies may be bought out, again turning earning assets in the form of stocks and bonds into cash that must be reinvested

Alternatively, we may need additional funds, perhaps for an emergency or to cover additional expenses, and we may not be capable of deciding which assets (stocks, corporate bonds, municipal bonds, government bonds) we should sell. Then there are periodic changes in tax laws such as the tax rates on dividends or capital gains which make some investments better for us than others.

And a safe company, whose stock has been known as suitable for "widows and orphans" for 100 years may suddenly change into a highly risky company, or vice versa.

Finally, many clients prefer a particular allocation of assets between stocks and bonds which reflects their preferences between safety and earning power. This balance may be 50/50, reflecting a fairly conservative approach, claimed to be suitable for those of retirement age (although at variance with this book which suggests taking virtually no risk for assets providing core income). Over time, the performance of the markets is likely to shift this balance away from the ideal. If stocks have a sudden run-up, the balance could shift to 60/40, and someone needs to "rebalance" the portfolio by selling some stocks and using the proceeds to buy bonds.

While most of these tasks are routine, almost mechanical, somebody must follow the portfolio on a fairly constant basis, probably at least quarterly, and have the knowhow and diligence to tweak it to best meet client needs. Some of us enjoy doing this work ourselves, just as some of us love to cook or tend our own yards or even fix our plumbing, and those of us who want to do it ourselves may be able to work through an on-line broker for very little money, as described in Chapter 5. However, others regard investment maintenance with distaste and would just as soon pay someone to do the work and make the decisions.

There are many products available that will do much of the routine work for us. Mutual funds, by law, diversify our investment into at least 20 different securities with a common purpose (such as growth, high tech, high dividends, utilities, etc.) so that if one security runs into difficulty, the other 19 are likely to help maintain our wealth. Jim feels that the professional investment analysts who work for the mutual funds, many with CFAs, are better equipped than he is to choose 20 or more companies into which clients' money can be invested. Therefore, he will recommend one or more mutual funds to his clients and will get a fee from each fund that his client buys.

To meet his clients' desires to grow their money in a safe way, he might buy two or more mutual funds for them; one could be a safe government bond fund and the other could be a stock fund. He could split the money 50/50 in the bond and stock mutual funds to take a middle ground between growth and safety, rebalancing the portfolio periodically as stocks go up or down in value relative to bonds. Alternatively, if he has a client whose core income falls short of her core retirement expenses but who wishes to take no risk with her financial assets, he could safely fund the deficit with a mutual fund made up of Treasury bonds, and let the rest of the money "ride" in growth stocks.

When I suggested an annuity to him he said "fine." A variable annuity would be one of the most profitable things he could sell to a customer, providing him with an upfront commission of about 5 percent of the client's investment. He had no interest, whatsoever, in selling an immediate fixed annuity to a client since it is tough to sell a fixed annuity and he would make very little on the sale, although he did say that an immediate fixed annuity would be a good idea for a person like myself who was knowledgeable and self-confident.

Once Jim's clients have been set up with the products they need, they are not going to talk much to him unless they need something or an event occurs, such as an economic downturn or a tax law change which causes Jim to suggest a revised strategy. While this is probably good for Jim's customers, it doesn't do much to generate additional income for Jim who generally makes money only when products are bought or sold.[68] However, Jim has been in the business a long time, isn't greedy, and has a lot of client wealth invested with him. Nearly every day he will get a call from a client who has accumulated some money to invest or who must sell some of his investments to cover expenses. This generates more than enough income for a person who has managed his own money well over a long, successful career.

Working with a Stockbroker

If you choose to deal directly with a stockbroker (registered representative) rather than through a financial advisor, you can maintain control of the account yourself, giving orders to the broker. Alternatively, you can give the broker legal trading authority over the account in which case the account becomes known as a discretionary account. As explained above, limited trading authority, through a limited power of attorney, allows your broker to buy or sell investments for you, using the money that is in your account, but does not allow the broker to take money or securities out of your account. If you want your broker to pay your bills and taxes for you, you generally have to give the broker full trading authority which allows them complete control over the money you have invested with them.

It is possible for you to work directly with a stockbroker to handle many of the routine financial tasks described in the previous section without handing them legal power to make your investments for you. For example, you could ask your broker to notify you whenever more than a specified amount of money, such as $5,000, accumulated in your account so that the broker could recommend a suitable investment for you. To make your life easier, you could also invest in stocks, mutual funds or ETF's (Exchange Traded Funds) that automatically reinvest your dividends for you so that you don't have to worry about making continual reinvestment decisions. You could also schedule a semi-annual or annual meeting with your broker, in person or by phone, to review your account and decide if and how it should be rebalanced.

The services that you can get from a "full-service" (as opposed to discount) stockbroker can generally be paid for in two ways – commissions based on the dollar amount of securities purchased or sold through your stockbroker, or a percent of total dollars that the stockbroker manages for you in a discretionary account. If you work with a stockbroker without giving him or her discretionary power to handle your investment decisions, you will pay for the service in the form of commissions. Without a discount, this will typically amount to about 2 percent of every purchase or sale of securities that you make.

If your account is sizeable, more than several hundred thousand dollars, you may be able to negotiate a discount of as much as 50-60 percent off the commission, taking it down to about 1 percent or less of your trades. If you have a million dollars invested and the broker recommends buying and selling 20 percent of it every year, it would amount to $400,000 in trades ($200,000 sold and $200,000 bought) which would cost you about $8,000 per year in commissions at regular rates without a discount. However, if the broker makes many trading recommendations and you buy and sell half your portfolio per year, undiscounted brokerage commissions could amount to $20,000 annually.

Commissions and Conflicts of Interests

It is clear that if you work with a stockbroker, financial planner or financial advisor on a commission basis, your interests may not be aligned with theirs. The more your portfolio is traded, the higher the commissions, which is almost always good for the money manager and bad for you. If you maintain control over your trades, you can limit the amount that you want to spend on commissions. If you give the broker discretionary power over your account, brokers can "churn" it with lots and lots of trades, turning *your* assets into *their* commissions. Even though "churning" per se is illegal, it is not easy to establish when the broker ceases trading for the good of the customer and begins trading for his or her own good. The brokerage firm has an obligation to monitor all discretionary accounts to prevent churning, yet the brokerage firm, which shares commissions with the broker, profits from high investment turnover. And besides, who is to say that 100 percent turnover per year is really "churning?" Many mutual funds have turnover rates that high or higher.

It should also be noted that you cannot sue your broker for harming you through excessive churning or for making investments that are not consistent with your age or risk preference. Instead you must submit your case to arbitration by an industry board. In order to open a brokerage account, you must waive your right to sue your broker in the future for anything the firm will do. This waiver has been upheld as legal by the courts.

Wrap Accounts

Noting the success of the financial advisors who make money by charging a fixed percentage of assets under management, brokers now offer "wrap accounts" which are discretionary accounts in which a fixed management fee is charged instead of commissions. This prevents the broker from "churning" your account to generate commission income. However, wrap accounts typically charge about 1.5 percent of the assets under management per year. If, like many folks in or near retirement, you have a conservative portfolio invested primarily in secure bonds which pay relatively little interest, this charge can equal a third or more of your total return.

The final 60 years of the 20th Century marked a period of amazing growth for the US as it transformed itself into the world's leading industrial economy. The stocks of the companies that powered this growth also increased dramatically, averaging a total return (with dividends) of about 11 percent per year.

Stocks have not done nearly as well in the 21st Century, with returns from 2000 through 2012 averaging closer to 5 percent than 11 percent. With aging populations, intense worldwide competition and large amounts of government debt weighing down the economies of the developed countries, few analysts believe that company stock can return to and maintain the (average) double digit returns of the last century. If returns on stock continue to be in the range of 5 percent, paying 1.5 percent for investment management takes nearly a third of total earnings from all-stock portfolios and a much higher proportion of the balanced portfolios of most older Americans which are made up of stocks and bonds.

Checking Out Possible Financial Advisors

While most financial advisors are honest, hardworking professionals, they are subject to a lot of temptations to make some "easy" money from vulnerable clients. Brokers can turn your money into commissions for themselves by trading your investments excessively (churning), and financial planners and investment advisors can sell you products with unusually high commissions or fees for themselves, or products that you don't really need. They can also invest your money in deals that benefit them or, worst of all, they can take your money and disappear.

The Federal Securities and Exchange Commission (SEC) suggests ways in which you can check out brokers and other financial advisors before committing your money to them:

"Federal or state securities laws require brokers, investment advisers, and their firms to be licensed or registered, and to make important information public. But it's up to you to find that information and use it to protect your investment dollars. The good news is that this information is easy to get, and one phone call or web search may save you from sending your money to a con artist, an unscrupulous financial professional, or a disreputable firm.

"Before you invest or pay for any investment advice, make sure your brokers, investment advisers, and investment adviser representatives have not had disciplinary problems or been in trouble with regulators or other investors. You also should check to see whether they are registered or licensed.

"This is very important, because if you do business with an unregistered securities broker or a firm that later goes out of business, there may be no way for you to recover your money — even if an arbitrator or a court rules in your favor."[69]

Checking Out Brokers and Brokerage Firms

To find out if brokers are properly licensed in your state and whether they have received serious complaints from investors or have had disciplinary problems with regulators, you can check them out through the FINRA Broker Check Search at http://brokercheck.finra.org/Search/Search.aspx. I checked out my own broker on this site and quickly found out that:

• He works for the large firm he says he works for and has for 30 years

• He is not currently suspended or inactive with any regulator

• There are no events disclosed about this broker which means that he is "clean." According to the web site, "Disclosure events are certain criminal matters; regulatory actions; civil judicial proceedings; customer complaints, arbitrations, or civil litigations; employment terminations; and financial matters in which the broker has been involved."

If I wanted, I could have downloaded a more detailed report about this broker by clicking a box. To make matters somewhat more difficult for consumers, the FINRA database has plenty of information about large multi-state or national brokerage firms but may not have investor complaints about a local brokerage firm which only operates in your state. You may have to contact your state securities regulator for that information, often by phone since they are reluctant to put that information online. The following web site gives you the contact information for your state: http://www.nasaa.org/about-us/contact-us/contact-your-regulator/

The value of Broker Check has recently been called into question as the result of brokers with client complaints being able to have them "expunged" or removed from their files in many cases. According to a June 2013 article in the *New York Times*, "Last year state regulators received 519 requests from brokers asking to be allowed to move forward with a panel's expungement recommendation, up from 110 in 2009."[70]

Finally, it is important to deal with a broker who is a member of SIPC, the Securities Investor Protection Corporation. They are the folks who insure your investments in stocks and bonds up to $500,000 if your brokerage firm goes belly up. You can check that your broker is a member of SIPC by entering the name in the web site http://www.sipc.org/Members/Database.

Checking Out Investment Advisers

If your potential investment advisor is not affiliated with a brokerage firm, it is now somewhat *more difficult* than it used to be to check that person out. The Dodd-Frank Act, which is generally regarded as consumer and investor friendly, actually excluded many investment advisors from having to register with the SEC. Formerly, investment advisory firms with $30 million or more of assets under management had to register with the SEC. Now, that lower limit has been moved up to $110 million. Firms smaller than that, which include many if not most local firms, have to register only with their states.

In order to find out information about investment advisors registered with the SEC, you should look through the advisor's client brochure. This summarizes much of the legally-required information in its registration form, called "Form ADV" which is generally available online through the SEC's web site http://www.adviserinfo.sec.gov/IAPD/Content/Search/iapd _Search.aspx . The brochure, which discloses fees and any disciplinary actions taken against the firm, should also have a brochure supplement that provides information about the employees of the advisor who actually deal with clients and provide investment advice. If they don't give you a client brochure, be suspicious!

Suppose that your investment advisor is not a registered broker but buys and sells securities for you through another company called a "clearing broker." To be eligible for up to $500,000 in insurance on your securities and cash in the brokerage account in the event that the broker fails, make sure that the clearing broker is a member of SIPC through http://www.sipc.org/Members/Database.

The name of the clearing broker can be found on the client brochure of your investment advisor.

Checking Out Financial Planners

If you decide to work with a financial planner who is affiliated with a broker, you can check him or her out through the FINRA database described above. If the planner is registered as an investment advisor, you can check out larger firms with the SEC and smaller firms with your state securities commissioner.

Before hiring a person claiming to be a Certified Financial Planner, you may want to see if they are in good standing by checking with the CFP Board. You can do this by entering their name, city and state at http://www.cfp.net/find/VerifyCertificationCFP.aspx. You can also find out whether any disciplinary procedures have been taken against them through http://www.cfp.net/learn/disciplineactions.asp. This may not be enough, however. Even genuine CFPs are not guaranteed to remain honest.

One of the most egregious allegations of fraud by a financial planner was a very recent one involving a former chairman of NAPFA (National Association of Personal Financial Advisors), the major fee-only financial planning group, which prides itself on its integrity. Mark Spangler was indicted in May, 2012 by a federal grand jury on charges that include investment adviser fraud, wire fraud and money laundering. The SEC said while Mr. Spangler told clients he would invest primarily in publicly-traded securities, he instead used $47.7 million their money to fund two startup companies that he or his firm owned, one of which is now bankrupt. He was accused of providing his clients with misleading financial statements and then could not return his clients' funds when asked.

132

A few years before, a former president of NAPFA was charged by the SEC with accepting about $1.24 million in kickbacks related to unregistered investment pools.[71] If you are going to let someone else manage your money for you, you can't be too careful about whom they are. Bernie Madoff swindled hundreds of investors, some fairly sophisticated, out of billions of dollars, through a combination of charm, connections and devious accounting.

As we mentioned earlier, you are given enhanced protection against fraud if you deal with a financial planner associated with a major brokerage firm since they have professional compliance officers and are audited regularly under the auspices of the SEC. In addition, these firms have deep pockets and you are very likely to be reimbursed if cheated by a financial planner working for the firm, although recovery of your funds could take years.

Succession

When we entrust our finances to a trustworthy planner, broker or advisor for the rest of our life, what happens when they retire or die? Does a relative or partner take over our account or is it "sold" to a new firm? This question is relevant whether we have given our financial advisor discretionary power to manage our finances (through power of attorney) or whether we still must approve all financial decisions ourselves.

If we have turned over discretionary management of our finances to a financial manager, such as a broker, planner or financial advisor, we do have some legal protection if our financial manager retires, sells or leaves the firm. This is because the power of attorney granting them the management of our investments generally needs to be amended and signed again to transfer discretionary power over our assets to another person.

Imagine the scenario, however, when that occurs. We get a letter from our long-time, trusted advisor thanking us for doing business with him for 30 years and telling us that his accounts are being taken over by his daughter or partner or associate who has been in the business for 5, 10 or 15 years. We are invited to meet our new advisor in person and told that there is some paperwork to fill out to transfer the account. What do we do then?

We could move our business to another financial advisor, but do we know any? We could meet with the suggested successor, but how can we make a judgment based on a half-hour meeting? We could check references but really, what will that tell us? In essence, if we live long enough, we are likely to outlive our trusted, long-term advisor, particularly if we choose one based upon long years of experience. And, at that point, do we really want to have to trust our future to somebody new? This is a serious risk connected with even the best and most trustworthy financial advisor one could have.

There is something else that you must know. When financial advisors are ready to retire, they will "sell" your account to their successors for a rather handsome fee. This will help them fund their retirement. A standard arrangement in much of the industry is a payment based on fees paid by the inherited clients (you) over the next 5 years. This often begins at 60 percent of first year fees, declining to 50 percent of year 2 fees, etc., generally totaling about 200 percent of total annual fees. If you pay a fee of 1.5 percent to your financial advisor for managing a million dollars for you, your account will be sold for about $30,000 when your advisor retires.[72] So you see, it is in your trusted advisor's best interest to say wonderful things about your new advisor.

134

Assets Under Management

A few months back I was being interviewed by a well-known personal finance writer for a new book that she was finishing. After discussing the subject that motivated her call – my research into financial education and why it has been ineffective in raising the financial literacy of high school students – we began discussing financial planners, particularly the very good ones that we have known. Both of us lamented their inaccessibility, at least to us, for the few times that we really needed to purchase their expertise. "I was willing to pay $500 an hour to help me think through an issue," she said, "but I couldn't find anyone competent to take my money – not at *any* price."

The problem is that virtually all competent, fee-only financial planners, wealth managers and increasingly brokers have a single objective – *AUM* or "assets under management." Simply stated, if you have $1 million in assets, (often the minimum account size they will take) they really, really want to "manage" those assets for you at the common industry rate of 1.5 percent per year. A little arithmetic tells us that 1.5 percent of $1 million is $15,000 per year for them, year after year, for doing very little work. After reading Chapter 3 of this book, we realize that this is a life annuity for *them*, based on your life.

If a 70 year old man with a $1 million portfolio has a life expectancy of 14 years, he can be expected to generate $210,000 in fees in that period of time if he pays the industry "standard" rate of 1 ½ percent per year.[73] Can you see why a competent planner will disdain your offer of $500 or even $1,000 an hour to solve a pressing financial problem? They'd rather solve your problem for "free" if you allow them to manage your money.

Asset-based fees bring in about 85 percent of advisory-firm revenue. [74] While advisors have some incentive to increase the size of the assets (and their income) by giving good advice, there are also potential conflicts of interest in this relationship. Attempts to grow client assets (to increase fees) may result in taking greater risk than clients would want. Alternatively, a planner may discourage actions in the client's interests that would take assets out of the account. As an example, an adviser might be tempted to advise a client not to pay off a mortgage or buy life insurance since that would leave the advisor with less money to manage.

As we have seen earlier, if you mention to your financial advisor that you are interested in an immediate annuity, be prepared for a *very* negative reaction since advisors make a very small commission for selling a competitively-priced product *and* the money used to buy the annuity diminishes the value of *their* annuity income for the rest of your life since it cuts into your assets under management. Financial planners who sell annuity products may agree that an annuity is a good idea, but they will probably try to sell you a *variable* annuity which gives them an upfront "load" fee of as much as 5 percent and recurring annual income as well. In addition to the added cost to you, most variable annuities won't give you much, if any, *guaranteed* lifetime income to cover the deficit in your core expenses.[75] Also, as mentioned in Chapter 3, you can cash in a variable annuity if someone persuades you to do so in your dotage. It just doesn't provide the guaranteed lifetime income of a single payment immediate fixed annuity.

Then there is the question of how much you pay per hour for the valuable council of your financial advisor. At a rate of $500 per hour, you would have to take up 30 hours per year to get advice worth the $15,000 in annual fees. Very few clients use this much time, year after year. When the market is doing well, as it has historically done about 3 of every 4 years prior to the year 2000, financial advisors field few calls and earn their fees for little work. When the market tanks, financial advisors pay their dues by reassuring clients that the market will eventually recover. There is actually little that the advisor can do for you in either instance.

Guaranteed Lifetime Income?

In the difficult financial times we have experienced over the past dozen years, even the best financial experts have had difficulty producing a consistent rate of return of more than about 6 percent. If the best security analysts, who generally earn millions of dollars per year in salary and bonus working for large investment companies, are unable to generate a reasonable and steady rate of return, could you expect your advisor to do better?

Cities across the United States, such as Detroit, have begun failing and declaring bankruptcy, in large part because of their employee pension plans. These are defined benefit plans (some with COLAs) which promise to pay employees an "annuity" for life. By law, these plans must hire actuaries to insure that the plans are fully funded and capable of making these promised lifetime payments.

Most of these plans have hired professional money managers, many with MBAs and CFA designations, to try to earn the rate of return "required" to fulfill pension commitments. They can afford to hire professional money managers because they have a lot of assets, hundreds of millions or even billions of dollars, and there are scale economies in hiring the best money managers. The plans specify an overall target rate of return which has generally been about 8 percent. Unfortunately, with a stock market that isn't much above 1999 levels and a bond market paying next to nothing, the professional money managers have not been able to produce an 8 percent return, or anything near that amount.

The majority of public pension funds are still basing their ability to pay future retirees on assumed investment earnings of 7 or 8 percent, a practice that New York Mayor Michael Bloomberg recently called "indefensible." The former Solomon Brothers investment banker who became one of the world's richest men by delivering financial data to professional investors added, "If I can give you one piece of financial advice: If somebody offers you a guaranteed 7 percent on your money for the rest of your life, you take it and just make sure the guy's name is not Madoff." [76] In fact, the National Association of State Retirement Administrators found that from 2000 to 2012, earnings on pension assets have averaged only 5.7 percent per year. [77] And don't forget, even that 5.7 percent is not guaranteed for any period of time.

If you want to get a set amount of income guaranteed for the rest of your life (or the life of a surviving spouse), the only way to do that is through a fixed annuity. As we saw in Chapter 3, you really can't buy an annuity now that will guarantee you a rate of return over your lifetime that is equal to the 5.7 percent per year that professionally managed retirement funds have averaged. At best, you may be able to get 2.5 percent, guaranteed, and probably less. However, depending on your age, this may translate into a guaranteed lifetime cash flow equal to 8 percent of your investment because much of that income is return of your principal – the money you have invested.

If you don't annuitize your investment, most studies suggest that the maximum amount that you can take out each year, and still have a 95 percent chance of not outliving the fluctuating value of your investments, is just 4 percent or about half of what a man could get from an annuity purchased at age 70. Some experts feel that in the current investment environment, even taking out 4 percent of your investments each year is a stretch.[78]

Beat the Market?

As we have seen, good financial advisors can do a lot for you. They can help you choose an asset allocation that meets your need for safety, income and tax efficiency. They can reinvest cash that accrues to your account through dividends, interest and return of principal through bond calls and stock buyouts. They can send regular income to your checking account and arrange for extra funds to meet emergencies. They can help you readjust your portfolio for changes in tax laws. These are all useful services.

The one thing that they can't do, however, is outperform the market on a regular basis. Unfortunately, claims that they can is the reason why many people choose their financial advisors. Nearly four decades of research by finance professors has shown that few if any investment professionals can outperform the market on a risk-adjusted basis. This finding applies as well to mutual funds which are run by top professionals making salaries in the millions of dollars. And you are unlikely to find this level of talent from your local financial advisor or stockbroker.

The reason why professionals cannot beat the market on a regular basis is that the market itself is run by professionals. If we look at the widely-followed Standard & Poor's index of the 500 firms with the greatest stock value (the "S&P 500"), we find that even the smallest of these firms is followed by dozens of well-educated analysts who study them daily and know nearly everything about them. In addition, a very large proportion of all stock trades are made by professionals who can trade massive amounts of stock, many times a day, in order to gain a penny or two per share based on new information that is always flowing out. Recently, huge computers owned by "algorithmic traders" have begun trading hundreds of billions of dollars each day at nearly the speed of light. Humans can't think that fast and are frozen out of these markets.

The good news is that you don't need a huge computer or a set of brilliant stock analysts to do nearly as well as they do, virtually for free! All you have to do is buy the entire market, or a tiny piece of it, and you will do as well as the market. And these days, it can be done for very little money.

The two least expensive ways of buying the market are through an S&P 500 index fund offered by a reliable low-cost (not-for-profit) company such as Vanguard, or through shares in an Exchange Traded Fund (ETF) purchased through an on-line or discount broker. Your total annual expenses may amount to a tenth of one percent per year or less, compared to 15 times that amount if you use most financial advisors, equity mutual funds or stockbroker wrap accounts.[79] Over the long run you will do exactly as well as the market before fees and a lot better after fees, without taking the added risk of losing a lot of your money by underperforming the market since you have "bought" the market with your index ETF. What you don't get is the handholding of a financial advisor who will perform all of the account maintenance chores mentioned above. It's a cost-benefit choice that you need to make.

Will They Tell Me When I Get Stupid?

Many seniors, who pay a financial planner, wealth manager or broker a percentage of their assets to manage their money, depend on these advisors to protect them and their families when they begin behaving erratically, making bad financial decisions. Unfortunately, money managers who serve as fiduciaries to their clients are constrained by privacy laws from revealing a client's actions to anyone, including the client's spouse or children, unless the client signs a waiver well in advance of deterioration.

This means that you should discuss with your advisor your own preferences as to who to notify if you appear to be losing mental capacity and what powers you want that person to have. Most financial planners, and many other advisors insist that you give them a signed "client engagement letter" that contains limits on what they can and cannot do. For example, you might specify that you want your investments to be "conservative," limited only to bonds of the US government and top-rated corporations as well as stocks of the 100 largest US companies. If you want to guarantee the core income that you need from your managed account, you could specify in writing that the objective of the account is to generate a very secure income equal to the amount needed (say, $25,000) from Treasury bonds, corporate and municipal bonds rated AA or above, and companies that have paid steady or increasing dividends for at least 20 years.

Therefore, if you suddenly call up and want to put all of your money into the initial public offering (IPO) of a high tech company with little track record, this divergence from the client engagement letter will allow the advisor to decline to follow the order and will signal that something strange may be happening with you, the client. If you have agreed to allow the advisor to contact the trustee that you have designated in the event that you are mentally impaired (temporarily or permanently), your wealth can be protected against yourself.

Tests of Cognition

As part of medical school training, most aspiring physicians are taught to give aging patients or those showing signs of possible mental impairment a simple "test" of cognitive status. There are several brief tests that can take as little as 5 minutes to administer. Among these, the mini mental state examination (MMSE) or Folstein test[80] is probably the most commonly used.

Dr. Richard Peterson, a psychiatrist who specializes in human financial behavior, recommends that financial advisors evaluate their older clients for signs of dementia on a regular basis. He gives a checklist that he feels advisors should utilize at least once a year for clients over 65 and as early as age 50 for clients with a family history of dementia or signs of cardiovascular disease such as stroke, heart attack or type 2 diabetes[81]. The checklist includes unusual behaviors such as memory lapses, emotional changes, difficulty doing simple math and problems recognizing familiar faces, places or events. If the client does show these unusual behaviors indicating possible mental impairment, Dr. Peterson suggests that a mini mental state examination be used to see if further action needs to be taken.

Working with a colleague who is a physician and an investor, I have come up with a sample list of investment-appropriate questions that you may wish to have asked to you by your broker or wealth advisor at least once a year or whenever your behavior appears to be "unusual." By including this in your client engagement letter, you can better protect your finances from your future, less competent self.

"At your request, we set up some protections for your account for your own safety. Perhaps you don't recall, but you asked us to have you provide the answers to the following questions. You also requested that if you made more than one error in answering these questions, we *not* carry out your trading or withdrawal requests. You have asked us to notify the trustee of your living will if you have difficulty answering these questions

In what city and state do you live?
In what year were you born?
What is your wife's (your) maiden name?
What is your current address?
What is your home phone number?
 I am going to ask you to remember three objects and ask you to tell me what they are after a few minutes -- wristwatch, pen, chair
What is today's date?
What is 99 divided by 3?
Who is the President of the United States?
What were the three objects I asked you to remember?"

While not all brokers or financial advisors will agree to such a specification in their client engagement letter, I have found some (mostly younger) wealth managers who eagerly embraced the concept and felt that their compliance departments would have no objections. To my mind, this flexibility is certainly a point in their favor when it comes to choosing (or changing) advisors.

"Know Your Customer" and "Suitability" Rules

How much protection can we expect to get from our broker, financial planner or investment advisor if we start to behave strangely with money we invest through them? This can be a lot, as noted above, if we specify in writing which investments are acceptable and unacceptable, or if they are willing to administer a MMSE-type test of our specification, such as the one given above. Or, we can expect virtually no protection from our future, diminished self if we make our own investment decisions, particularly if we place our orders online.

Investment advisors, including those who work for brokerage firms, have *fiduciary obligations* to their customers which means that they are legally required to act for their benefit. Brokers who are not investment advisors have smaller obligations to act in the best interests of their customers although many large, retail brokerage firms have made all of their brokers *registered investment advisors* which obligates them to the same standards. On July 9, 2012, FINRA, the organization that regulates most brokers, adopted two revised rules specifying brokers' obligations to act in the best interests of their customers. Rule 2090 is the new "Know Your Customer" rule and Rule 2111 is the new "suitability" rule.

The rules basically say that a broker must know a sufficient amount of information about a client (such as age, other investments, financial situation, tax status, investment objectives, investment experience, liquidity needs, and risk tolerance) in order to *suggest* a suitable investment. While the new rules specifically include discretionary accounts managed by the broker, they do not appear to include unsolicited orders given by the client to a broker, a discount broker or an online broker.

Therefore, if you have traditionally managed your own investments and do not ask the broker for advice, and one day your investment behavior begins to diverge wildly from what it had been, your broker may have no legal obligation to discourage your actions, no matter how bizarre or destructive. Consequently, you may wish to find out if your broker is an investment advisor. If this is the case, you will have more legal protection if the broker carries out your irrational and unsuitable order.

If you find a broker who is an investment advisor, you might find it worthwhile to explore discounted rates (generally less than 1 percent) to transact with that human broker who is legally obligated to reject unsuitable orders from you. Contrast that with the less-expensive method of trading online, which offers no legal protection to you for unsuitable or irrational orders, and see whether the "insurance" against irrational orders is worth the added cost. This may be particularly valuable to you if you are a "buy and hold investor" who doesn't turn over much of your portfolio each year and won't generate huge commissions for the broker.

Conclusion

This chapter has looked at the ways we can turn over some or all of our financial decision-making to others and the qualifications they may have to give us advice and handle our money. It also examined how they are compensated for helping to manage our money and whether their incentives are aligned with ours.

Trust in professional financial advisors is widespread, with nearly three-quarters of US retail investors seeking advice from a financial adviser before purchasing shares. These advisors may be stockbrokers, financial planners or investment advisors or, more commonly, some combination of the three. There is some added protection that comes from using a financial advisor who works for a brokerage firm since brokerage firms are much more tightly regulated and examined than investment advisors and financial planners who do not work for brokerage firms. Larger, nationwide brokerage firms may offer additional protection for your investments since they have deep pockets in the event that your financial advisor absconds with your money. Some are so large that they are deemed by the government as "too big to fail."

There are three basic ways in which you can pay for the services of your financial advisor: a fee by the hour as you might pay an attorney or accountant, a commission based on the products that you buy, or a percentage of the assets that the advisor manages for you. Many consumers give discretionary power to their financial advisors (through a power of attorney) to buy and sell investments for them.

While there are many legitimate services that a financial advisor can provide for you, such as helping you to understand your retirement needs, your tax situation and securities that are best suited to your personality, too many advisors try to convince their customers that they have the ability to beat the market. This is a fallacy -- nobody beats the market, consistently and legally, particularly after the advisor's fee is subtracted from your return. We can do as well as the market through buying and holding stock indexes that are both inexpensive and widely available.

It is possible that if you work with a stockbroker, financial planner or financial advisor on a commission basis, your interests may not be aligned. For example, the more your portfolio is traded, the higher the commissions, which is almost always good for the financial professional and bad for you. If you give your broker discretionary power over your account, the broker can "churn" it to generate commissions. Even though "churning" is illegal, it is difficult to catch and easy for the broker to explain away.

Noting the success of the financial advisors who make money by charging a fixed percentage of assets under management, brokers now offer "wrap accounts" which are discretionary accounts for which a fixed management fee is charged instead of commissions. While this discourages the broker from "churning" your account to generate commission income, you are likely to be charged about 1 ½ percent of the assets that the broker manages which will eat up a large proportion of your annual return in a low-return era.

Many seniors, who pay a financial advisor a percentage of their assets to manage their money, depend on these advisors to protect them and their families when they begin behaving erratically, making bad financial decisions. Unfortunately, money managers who serve as fiduciaries to their clients are constrained by privacy laws from revealing the clients' actions to anyone, including the client's spouse or children, unless the clients sign a waiver well in advance of their deterioration

Erratic behavior, consistent with age-related cognitive decline, can be more easily detected and addressed if you give your financial professional a signed "client engagement letter" that contains limits on what they can and cannot do for you, even at your request. Therefore, if you suddenly call up and want to put all of your money into the initial public offering (IPO) of Facebook, this divergence from the client engagement letter will allow the advisor to decline to follow the order and will signal that something strange may be happening with you, the client. If you have agreed to allow the advisor to contact the trustee that you have designated in the event that you are mentally impaired (temporarily or permanently), your wealth can be protected against yourself. However, client engagement letters are typically used only in conjunction with powers of attorney granted to the financial professional to make decisions for you. If you choose to place your own orders, you are given little or no protection against your diminished future self.

What to Do When I Get Stupid

Chapter 5
What to Do *Before* I Get Stupid:
A Practical Review

At a Glance

In this chapter we attempt to provide practical solutions to the two major questions posed in the book:

Will I have sufficient guaranteed real income to last the rest of my life, no matter how long I live, and, if not, what can I do about it?

How can I protect my lifetime income against possible irrational decisions of my future self?

Those who find themselves without sufficient guaranteed lifetime income to maintain their current standard of living may have sufficient financial assets to remedy this situation. If they lack both sufficient lifetime income and the assets needed to provide this income, they have no choice but to modify their living standard.

To review, the easiest, safest, and least expensive way to turn financial assets into guaranteed lifetime income is through an immediate annuity. Immediate annuities are easy to understand products which may be purchased online or by phone from many life insurance companies. The market for immediate annuities is highly competitive, which benefits the buyers. Websites provide quotes from many different companies, enabling you to choose the one that pays the greatest monthly amount, for life, for a given investment. While most immediate annuities pay a fixed amount of money per month for life, you can also buy those that adjust automatically with the cost of living. Inflation-adjusted immediate annuities pay out less at first for a given investment to enable them to pay out more in the future when prices are higher.

Those who have sufficient pension or other fixed income may be able to protect that income against inflation by holding Treasury Inflation Protected Securities (TIPS). This chapter will give you an estimate of the amount of TIPS that you need to protect your pension against various possible levels of inflation.

The second part of this chapter deals with the practicalities of protecting your lifetime income against the possible irrational decisions of your future self. It does so using three possible ways in which you may wish to have your investments managed: managing them yourself through on online or discount broker, managing them through a full-service broker who will make recommendations to you or having them managed for you by a broker, planner or other type of investment manager.

Everyone should have a living will which, among other things, designates a trustee who can take care of your financial affairs if you are physically or mentally incapacitated. The addition of a Trust Protector to watch over your trustee can give you added assurance that your designated trustee is doing an honest, capable job of looking after your interests.

What happens when you no longer have the ability to manage your own finances in a rational fashion? If you have chosen to have a competent and trustworthy advisor manage them for you, your troubles are minimized. If, however, you have chosen to manage them yourself, you have a bigger problem if you become irrational or easily persuadable in the future. This is particularly true if you manage your investments online or through a discount broker who merely takes orders over the telephone. You may get some legal protection from a full-service broker since that person is subject to "know your customer' and "suitability" rules. It turns out that your "protection" becomes questionable if you place "unsolicited" orders that you have come up with yourself rather than take suggestions from your broker. If your broker is also a registered investment advisor, you may get an added layer of protection since he or she has a fiduciary obligation to look after your best interests. However, brokers may *still execute your unsolicited orders even if they are irrational or not in your best interests*. Therefore, you should try to get your broker, in advance, to agree to refuse unsolicited orders that are not consistent with your needs or your pattern of orders in the past.

There are a few ways in which you can try to protect your assets against irrational judgments that you might make. These include setting up a joint account which requires two approvals for purchase and sale of securities, splitting the assets between two accounts, one controlled by each party making up a couple, or even dividing up the password of an online account to make it difficult to make changes in it.

There are also a number of ways to set up accounts so that they need little management but will meet your needs for cash flow and safety. If accounts need little management, it is likely that you will pay little or no attention to them which minimizes the probability that you will screw them up. These methods are described later in this chapter.

Finally, many people can benefit from giving control of their assets to an honest and competent money manager. This can be costly, as much as 1.5 percent or more of your assets per year, but it can be a good value for those who lack the ability to do it themselves. The chapter contains a list of things that a good money manager can and should do for you. Before you choose to go this route, establish in writing that the money manager will perform these services and make sure that the fees are reasonable and well-understood.

Some Action Items

To repeat, the two major questions posed in the book ask us how we can generate sufficient guaranteed real income to last the rest of our lives, no matter how long we live and what are the best ways to protect our lifetime income against possible irrational decisions of our future selves. We must answer the second question regardless of how we choose to manage our finances: by ourselves at the lowest possible cost, with advice from a commissioned broker or in the control of an investment manager?

While the questions may appear to be simple, the answers are anything but. We all have different situations and may need to focus on specific parts of the questions that are most relevant to our situation. For example the first question asks how we can generate sufficient guaranteed real income to last the rest of our lives, no matter how long we live. This question may pose no problem to a few of us, but some of us may be short on income, short on guaranteed income, short on real, inflation-adjusted income, or short on lifetime income. If we are short on income, we may have financial assets that can be used to increase our guaranteed lifetime income or, if not, we have to consider an alternative solution. Finally, we may have sufficient guaranteed lifetime income, but some of it may not be protected against inflation.

To help understand the ways in which we must approach these questions, a logical diagram has been provided for each question. The way to use the diagram is to begin at the top with a yes or no answer to the overall question. You may find it useful to choose the response under each answer that is closest to your own situation, and you will find that it leads to a set of possible solutions to your problems. The solutions will be discussed in greater detail in this chapter.

1. Will you have sufficient guaranteed real income to last the rest of your life, no matter how long you live?

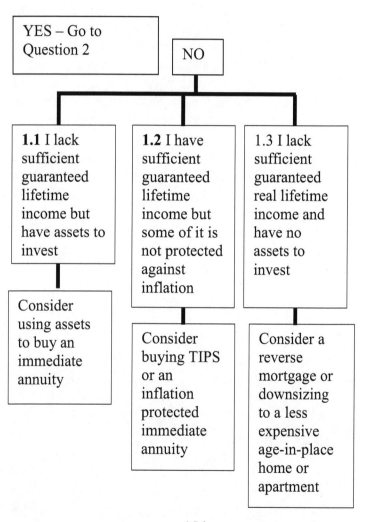

YES – Go to Question 2

NO

1.1 I lack sufficient guaranteed lifetime income but have assets to invest

Consider using assets to buy an immediate annuity

1.2 I have sufficient guaranteed lifetime income but some of it is not protected against inflation

Consider buying TIPS or an inflation protected immediate annuity

1.3 I lack sufficient guaranteed real lifetime income and have no assets to invest

Consider a reverse mortgage or downsizing to a less expensive age-in-place home or apartment

If you answered yes to question one, that is terrific. It means that you are very likely to be able to live with the rest of your life, no matter how long you live, in reasonable comfort, without having to significantly alter your lifestyle. You may want to move on to Question 2 which deals with protecting yourself against your future, perhaps irrational, self.

If you answered "no" to question one, you either have a shortage of guaranteed lifetime income or find that some of your guaranteed lifetime income is not "real" or guaranteed against inflation. Let's begin with those who have a shortage of guaranteed lifetime income. We will worry about inflation protection in a little while.

Folks who are short of guaranteed lifetime income fall into two possible categories – those who have sufficient financial assets to buy needed guaranteed lifetime income, and those who have neither the needed income nor the assets that can purchase the income they need for the rest of their lives.

1.1 I Lack Sufficient Guaranteed Lifetime Income But Have Assets to Invest

In Chapter Three we learned that the easiest, safest, and least expensive way to turn financial assets into guaranteed lifetime income is through an immediate annuity. How do you go about purchasing an immediate annuity? Let's review the general principles that we've learned and see how we can apply them.

It may not be prudent to begin by asking this question of your broker, financial planner, wealth manager, or insurance sales person. Their interests may not be aligned with yours. If you use some of the funds that they now manage for you, this action will deprive them of some annual income. As an example, if they charge you a common rate of 1.5 percent per year of assets under management, for every $100,000 that you take from your account to purchase an annuity, you are depriving them of *their* annuity of $1,500 per year! If your life expectancy is 15 years, this is currently worth $18,572 to them (present discounted value at current 10 year Treasury note rates of about 2.5 percent[82]). And if they manage your money on a commission basis, then the money you use to purchase your annuity is money that will no longer generate commissions for them. Ultimately, when you've done the necessary research suggested in this chapter, you may wish to circle back to them as an informed consumer to see if they can meet your specific product needs at a reasonable cost.

Of course, if you ignore this warning and go directly to your financial adviser and tell him or her that you are interested in an annuity, they're likely to be delighted. Chances are good that they will try to sell you a *variable* annuity which, unlike a fixed annuity, does not guarantee a dependable income for life. A variable annuity is a combination of a mutual fund and an insurance product. The amount of income that they pay for the rest of your life depends upon how well the securities in the mutual fund do. If your variable annuity contains stocks and the market goes up, the amount of your annual payment will also go up. However, if there is a sizable market collapse, you may find that your payments can fall with the fall in the market.

Aside from being risky, a variable annuity is generally burdened with very high fees. Some of these fees are charged by the insurance company who issues the variable annuity because they not only have to manage an insurance product (the annuity), but they also need to pay the folks who manage the mutual fund. The better known the name of the mutual fund associated with the variable annuity, the more you will have to pay, since the fund's reputation depends in large part on the amount of

156

advertising they do.   Insurance companies that issue variable annuities associated with widely-advertised mutual funds generally pay the mutual fund 50 basis points (1/2 of 1 percent).   Then they mark that up two or three times before adding their own insurance charges and generous sales commissions.   Total charges for "brand-name" variable annuities can reach 3 percent or more per year.

Also, please remember, that variable annuities, like all discretionary insurance products, are *sold,* not bought. In order to give a financial adviser the incentive to sell a complex product like a variable annuity, insurance companies generally provide that advisor with a large upfront commission of 5 percent or more in addition to an annual payment based upon the size of the annuity.

Immediate annuities, on the other hand, are plain vanilla products often sold directly to the consumer by almost every insurance company.   In economics, a similar product that is sold by many different companies is generally called a "commodity."   Since there is little to distinguish the immediate annuity of one company from that of another company, consumers tend to buy annuities, like all commodities, on the basis of price.   This tends to take away the ability of any single company to charge a much higher price for the product since consumers choose largely by price.   Fortunately, there are websites that provided quotes from many different companies.   We will show you, below, exactly how to use the web site to find out the cost of an immediate annuity necessary to make up the shortfall in your guaranteed lifetime income.

Finding Annuity Costs

In April 2013, having passed my 70th birthday, I went online to www.immediateannuities.com, entered (anonymously) my birthday, gender and state and the amount I wished to invest in an immediate annuity (I entered $100,000). Instantly, I found that I could get $638.26 per month for the rest of my life which is equal to $7,659 per year on a "single life annuity" with no payments to beneficiaries. If I entered the age of my wife and the proportion of my payment we wished her to have if I died first, it would have recalculated my payment. The younger my wife, the smaller the amount that I would have received.

Since this was all done anonymously, immediateannuities.com could not give me a written, binding quote. Therefore, I gave them my name and address and a day or so later received written quotes from the eleven insurance companies that would pay me the greatest monthly, lifetime payment. Those quotes were mostly binding for a week although a couple were binding for two weeks. The companies were all giants in the life insurance industry including MetLife, New York Life and Nationwide. All of my quotes came from companies that had high A.M. Best ratings of A, A+ or A++. The current ratings of the insurers were included with the booklet of quotes.

True to its promise, I was not contacted again by immediateannuities.com to buy an annuity. However, I had questions and called the company and was put through to Hersh Stern, its founder and general agent for 21 life insurance companies who offer immediate annuities. He is licensed to sell these annuities in all 50 states plus the District of Columbia. When I asked about immediate annuities that adjusted to changes in inflation, he sent me, via email, a quote from American General which offered such a policy and which I described in Chapter 3.

Even if you have a broker, planner or wealth manager to whom you are loyal, I would urge you to go to immediateannuities.com to check out the best monthly income that you can receive for a set investment (I always use $100,000 for purpose of comparison). Then you can call other companies, brokers or wealth managers and see how they compare. It doesn't cost you anything to get a quote; you can do it in a few minutes and you don't even have to reveal your identity.

1.2 I Have Sufficient Guaranteed Lifetime Income But Some Is Not Protected Against Inflation

Some of us are fortunate enough to have sufficient regular income to meet our retirement needs. However, a portion of our needed income may not be protected against inflation. This will be the case if we have a defined benefit pension without a cost-of-living adjustment or if we are dependent on interest from bonds or other types of regular fixed-income investments. In this section we will learn how to make our needed retirement income increase with inflation.

Many of us receive part of our core retirement income from dividends on the stocks that we own. Clearly this income is neither as safe from default as interest on Treasury bonds nor as safe from inflation as an investment in Treasury Inflation Protected Securities. Stock prices and dividends, in general, tend to adjust to stable rates of inflation over time but often do poorly when inflation is sudden or unanticipated. However, investments in the stocks of well-established, highly-rated companies with a long record of paying reliable dividends that increase over time may be something that we can consider. The stocks of such "widows and orphans" companies tend to pay relatively high dividends for two reasons. First, they are generally stocks of companies with stable, dependable businesses, such as utilities who can sell their products in both good and bad times. Second, the demand for these stocks by those who seek reliable, but unspectacular income makes older investors their primary owners. This, so-called "clientele effect" generally prevents the companies from changing their business models or altering their stream of dividend payments.

During periods of inflation, utility stocks also tend to do relatively well since many are monopolies with the power to raise prices as their costs rise. This enables them to maintain or even increase dividend payments as consumer prices go up. Therefore, a diversified portfolio of such stocks, in a low-cost mutual fund or ETF, while not 100 percent safe, may be a reasonable way to protect core retirement income from both economic turndowns and the effects of inflation.

If we don't trust the stock market to give us reliable, inflation-protected retirement income, perhaps the simplest way to lock in such income is to buy an immediate annuity that adjusts to inflation. As we have seen in Chapter 3, adding the inflation adjustment will cost me (male, age 70) more than a third of the payment that I would receive from an immediate annuity without this benefit. Therefore, my decision must be based on the overall exposure that I have to inflation and the degree to which my financial situation can adjust to it. If I have great exposure to inflation, an inflation-adjusted annuity may be worth the cost

Converting Fixed to Inflatable Income

In Chapter 2 we mentioned that those who had enough nominal income to fund core retirement expenses, but not enough inflation-adjusted income, could cover the inflation gap by holding a sufficient amount of Treasury Inflation Protected Securities ("TIPS"). Here we will give you an estimate of how much of an investment you will have to make in TIPS bonds.

As an example, suppose that Jill has $55,000 in inflatable core retirement expenses and gets $35,000 per year in Social Security retirement benefits. This leaves her with a deficit of $20,000 ($55,000 minus $35,000) in inflatable, lifetime income which she has to make up. If Jill has a defined benefit pension of $20,000 with a Cost of Living Adjustment (COLA), she is all set.

Suppose, however, that Jill has a defined benefit pension of $20,000 per year *without* a COLA. Her only deficit now is the potential loss of purchasing power on her $20,000 annual pension due to future inflation. Her situation is illustrated in Chart 5-1.

The loss of a cost of living adjustment to a pension may not appear to amount to much. At recent inflation rates of just about 2 percent per year, Jill's loss of purchasing power on a fixed payment of $20,000 per year would just be $400 the first year ($20,000 times 2 percent). However, 30 years from now (if Jill lives this long), inflation of just 2 percent per year compounded for 30 years would result in prices 81 percent higher than they are now[83] and Jill's $20,000 annual pension payment would be able to purchase just $11,050 worth of goods, measured in today's prices. This is a big time reduction in purchasing power!

If Jill has the assets, she may be able to protect herself by buying inflation-protected Treasury bonds, "TIPS." Not only are these 100 percent safe if held to maturity, they also increase in value with inflation.[84]

In this book, we have spoken often of TIPS. To see how they can protect your regular income against inflation, we must understand exactly how they work. At the basic level they work like every other Treasury bond in that they pay a stated rate of interest on the amount that you have invested. If you buy a regular Treasury bond that has a yield of 2 percent and a face value of $1,000, that bond will pay you 2 percent of the face value ($20) per year until it

Chart 1
Jill has $20,000 in Core Income that is Not Inflatable

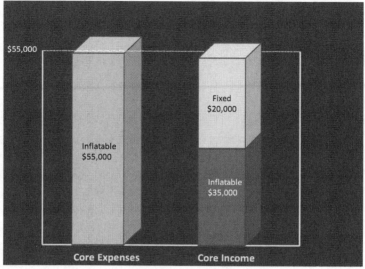

matures at which time it will repay the face value ($1,000) to you. The only difference with TIPS is that the face value of the bond increases with the rate of inflation.

If you invest $1,000 in a 30-year TIPS bond with a rate of return of 2 percent of the face value, the face value will increase with inflation which means that the value of the 2 percent interest will *also increase with inflation.* If inflation the first year is 5 percent, the face value of the bond will increase by 5 percent to $1,050 at the end of the year. In the second year, you will be paid 2 percent of this increased amount or $21 in interest.[85] Your total return for the first year includes the $50 increase in the face value of your bond and the $20 in interest for a total of $70 or 7 percent of your initial investment of $1,000.

162

When the TIPS bond matures, you get the inflation-adjusted face value which is likely to be much greater than what you paid for the bond. You can also sell your TIPS bond at any time for close to its adjusted face value in the "secondary market" since there are always a lot of investors who want to buy TIPS. Much, if not most of the return you get on TIPS is the amount added to the face value of the bond as the result of inflation, to compensate for lost purchasing power on your nominal retirement income. It will be necessary for you to periodically sell some of your TIPS. If consumer prices increase by 5 percent the first year after you invested in TIPS, you need to realize TIPS income equal to 5 percent of your unprotected income. If you are trying to protect a pension of $10,000 per year, you would need to generate $500 from your TIPS. If there isn't sufficient interest generated by the TIPS, you will need to sell enough to make up the difference.

The amount of TIPS that you need to cover your loss in purchasing power due to inflation varies with the *average* rate of inflation expected over the next 30 years as well as with the real rate of return paid on the TIPS when you buy them. At current expected average inflation[86] rates (over the next 30 years) of 2 percent, you would need to buy $52,257 in TIPS to cover the anticipated loss in purchasing power of a $10,000 fixed pension over 30 years[87]. At a 4 percent expected rate of inflation, you would need to purchase $88,703 in TIPS. Table 5-1, below, estimates the amount of 30-year TIPS you must hold to offset purchasing power loss of $10,000 per year for 30 years.

Table 1
Amount of 30-Year TIPS Needed to Offset Inflation
Risk to a Payment of $10,000 per Year at Real Rates of
2%

Average Inflation	TIPS Needed
2%	$52,257
3.43%	79,553
4%	88,703
5.44%	108,378
6%	114,913
8%	134,326

Note: This table provides the author's estimate of the investment in 30 year TIPS with a yield of 2% needed to offset *average* rates of inflation over that time on an annual payment of $10,000. Calculations underlying this table are complex and assume that the entire investment in TIPS will be used up (sold or matured) in 30 years.

For a little perspective, inflation in the US over the past century (since 1913) has averaged 3.43 percent[88] although the highest 30-year rate of inflation since the Second World War was 5.44 percent from 1966-1995[89]. Inflation is not politically popular and the Federal Reserve is specifically charged with keeping it low. Therefore, high rates are not very likely over 30 years, although they did go into double digits for a few years in the early 1980s before dropping sharply.

Table 1 uses the real rate of 2 percent which has been the historical average rate on 30 year TIPS. While this rate has fallen to as little of .5 percent as the result of quantitative easing by the Federal Reserve in 2012, it was back up to nearly 1.5 percent by mid-year 2013. The table uses several different rates of average inflation over 30 years, ranging from 2 percent to 8 percent. It also includes 3.43 percent which is the average rate over the past century and 5.44 percent which has been the *highest* 30 year average since the end of the Second World War. Note that these calculations amortize or use up the value of your investment over 30 years so that, at the end of this period, your TIPS are totally exhausted, if you live so long.

If, for example, you want to buy inflation protection on $10,000 in income and you feel that it is unlikely that inflation will *average* more than the current rate of 2 percent over the next 30 years (although it could be higher for some of those years), you would only have to buy $52,257 in 30 year TIPS. However, if you wanted to insure your purchasing power to the *average* inflation of 3.43 percent per year over the past century, you would need to invest $79,553 in TIPS. If you underestimate average 30-year inflation by a little, your TIPS will largely cover you.

Returning to the example of Jill who lacks $20,000 in inflation protection from her pension, she can fully insure that $20,000 against average inflation of up to 3.43% (the average rate over the past century) rate) for a $159,106 investment in 30-year TIPS paying 2 percent (2 times $79,553). Since current rates on 30 year TIPS are still below 2 percent, Jill may decide to "ladder" her investment by buying some TIPS now (perhaps a third of what she needs) and some in a year and in two years to take advantage of higher rates expected as the Fed relaxes its quantitative easing.

TIPS Versus Inflatable Annuity

In Chapter 3 we showed that in early 2013 a 70 year old man could purchase $7,149 in annual lifetime income that was not inflation-adjusted for $100,000. The same $100,000 would purchase $5,241 in inflation-adjusted income. By using some simple arithmetic, the cost of **$10,000** in inflation-adjusted lifetime income would be

$190,803[90] while the cost of $10,000 in non-inflation-adjusted lifetime income would be $139,879[91]. The difference is $50,924 which is the cost of protecting the $10,000 payment against inflation for life (about 13 years).

The large cost needed to insure a $10,000 annual payment against the ravages of inflation helps us understand several valuable points. First, we should thank our lucky stars every day for the inflation protection provided by Social Security (or defined benefit COLAs if we should be so fortunate). If we have a life expectancy of 13 years and get Social Security retirement benefits of $30,000 per year, the value of the cost-of-living adjustment alone is worth about $153 thousand in today's dollars[92]. Medicare is also protected against medical inflation which has been much higher than consumer price inflation in most recent years. Second, if we are not yet retired, the 8 percent addition to our Social Security retirement benefits for each year we wait to accept payments after reaching full retirement age (currently 66) and until age 70, is *fully* protected against inflation, making it that much more valuable.

Table 1 tells us that an investment in TIPS of $52,257 will protect the $10,000 annual payment against inflation for 30 years if inflation averages 2 percent per year. This is slightly more than the $50,924 additional investment needed to buy an inflation-adjusted single payment immediate annuity which will protect the same $10,000 annual payment against inflation for life. The inflation-adjusted annuity would appear to be the better deal since it lasts for life (and not just 30 years) and will protect against average inflation rates of more than 2 percent. However, to my knowledge you can't buy that part of an annuity that will just provide you with inflation protection on a nominal payment and not also buy the nominal annuity payment, so you have to concoct your own protection. In addition, the TIPS have the advantage of leaving something to your estate if you die in less than 30 years (a 70 year old man is expected to die in about 13 years) while the single payment immediate annuity will not, unless there are survivor benefits.

There are two problems connected with using TIPS to inflation-protect lifetime income, however. First, you are protected only against average rates of inflation that resemble those of the past and *not* against sustained, high rates of inflation approaching 10 percent or more. Second, 30 year TIPS (the longest maturity TIPS available) protect your income for only 30 years. If a 70 year old lives to be older than 100, (or a 60 year-old lives longer than 90, which is a real possibility) the inflation protection will cease since the TIPS will have been used up. If that is a real concern, an additional deferred annuity that begins at age 90 or 100 could be purchased for a relatively small amount of money.

The takeaway is that it is cumbersome, expensive and imprecise to inflation-proof your nominal retirement income. If some of your inflatable retirement expenses are covered by non-inflation-adjusted sources of income, it may be worthwhile to consider buying some TIPS if you have the financial resources to do so. And while dividends on stocks will often adjust to gradual increases in inflation, high rates of inflation often cause stock values to decrease in fear of an unstable economy. This is the reason why I include TIPS in my investment portfolio. It gives me a good return on a very safe investment and it provides me with insurance in case inflation flares up again.

1.3 I Am Short on Guaranteed Real Lifetime Income and Have No Financial Assets

If your core retirement income is not high enough to support your basic standard of living for the rest of your life, and you do not have the financial assets to purchase additional lifetime income through an annuity, there are basically just two things that you can do. Both alternatives have been covered in earlier chapters.

If you have substantial untapped equity in your home, you can turn that equity into lifetime income through a reverse mortgage and the purchase of an immediate annuity. The annuity you purchase can be fixed if relatively few of your expenses are inflatable, or it can be inflation-protected if you are willing to accept the lower annual return that comes with inflation-protection. Go back and read about government-guaranteed and approved reverse mortgages in Chapter 3 of this book.

If you do not have a lot of equity in your home as the result of the recent fall in home values or because you have already taken out much of the equity in a home equity loan or line of credit (or perhaps because you don't own a home), you have little choice but to cut your core expenses. For most people, the largest single expense relates to their home which implies some downsizing.

Chapter 2 covers the importance of having an age-in-place home which doesn't have to be expensive. With the aging of the American population, many age-in-place apartments or condominiums have been built for older folks who are willing to trade off square footage and private amenities for a smaller, safer place.

2. Is your lifetime income protected against possible irrational decisions of your future self?

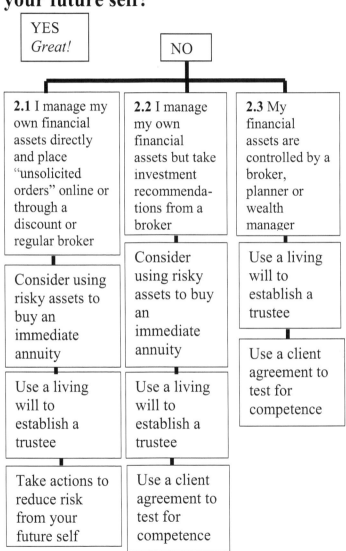

YES
Great!

NO

2.1 I manage my own financial assets directly and place "unsolicited orders" online or through a discount or regular broker

Consider using risky assets to buy an immediate annuity

Use a living will to establish a trustee

Take actions to reduce risk from your future self

2.2 I manage my own financial assets but take investment recommendations from a broker

Consider using risky assets to buy an immediate annuity

Use a living will to establish a trustee

Use a client agreement to test for competence

2.3 My financial assets are controlled by a broker, planner or wealth manager

Use a living will to establish a trustee

Use a client agreement to test for competence

If you answered "yes" to Question 2, your lifetime income is protected against possible irrational decisions of your future self, it means that you have thought through the ramifications of age-related cognitive decline very carefully and have taken actions to protect your lifetime income against them. These actions may include having sufficient Social Security or pension income, supplemented, perhaps with an immediate life annuity. Alternatively, you may have placed your financial assets in a trust with a reputable bank with long experience in managing financial assets. If you answered "no" to Question 2, you have some issues to resolve. The best way to address them is to decide which branch of the decision tree is most relevant to you:

1.   You manage your own financial assets directly, either online or through a discount or full service broker, by placing "unsolicited orders" for investment decisions that you have made.

2.   You manage your own financial assets indirectly by first discussing your needs with a broker, planner or wealth manager and then deciding to take some or all of their recommendations

3.   You do not manage your own financial assets since you have given power of attorney to your broker, planner or wealth manager to control your assets.

Establishing a Trustee

Regardless of how you choose to manage your financial assets, it is important to have a living will which specifies a trustee who will take over management of your finances in the event that you are no longer competent to manage them yourself. The trustee could be a dependable and knowledgeable child, spouse, relative or friend or it could be a professional trustee, perhaps from the trust department of a reputable bank.

When you work with your attorney to draw up your will, he or she will point out to you the importance of selecting an honest and reliable trustee who will insure your welfare if you are alive but disabled and who will fairly distribute your assets, in accordance with your will, after your death.

Trust Protector

Unfortunately, there is always the possibility that your designated trustee turns out to not be very trustworthy. This can happen for many reasons, including a trustee's illness, changed circumstances or even an unknown drug problem. If trustees really want to get control of your assets, they can try to have you declared mentally unfit to manage your own finances, leaving your assets in their hands. While they cannot legally take your assets, they can pay themselves large fees to "manage" your affairs and even buy themselves cars and houses to "help them help you." In short, there are many ways in which they can use up your remaining assets while you are alive and use the remaining assets to benefit themselves after your death.

To safeguard yourself and your estate from a dishonest or unreliable trustee, ask your estate attorney about a "Trust Protector," often just called a "Protector," whose job it is to make sure that your trustee is doing his or her job honestly or competently.[93] The protector could be a friend or relative or it could be a professional, such as an attorney who is paid for this service. The primary power of the protector is to be able to fire the existing trustee, if necessary. A successor trustee can be named in your will as a "backup," or appointed by the court, if you don't want to give the protector the right to name a successor trustee. To prevent conflicts of interest, the protector can generally not name him or herself as the successor trustee.

2.1 I Manage My Own Financial Assets Directly

If you manage your own investments, either online or by giving verbal orders to a human discount or full-service broker, you have little legal protection against irrational decisions that you may make in the future. As mentioned earlier, the "know your customer rule" which demands that brokers "recommend" only those investments that are compatible with the customer's needs, does not generally cover unsolicited (i.e.,unrecommended) customer orders. In fact, if you place an unsolicited order with a broker, the confirmation slip will indicate that the order is unsolicited. This protects the broker from lawsuits alleging that the order did not meet the customer's needs.

It is virtually impossible to prevent the execution of an irrational online order since one of the benefits of online trading is the speed of execution, often a second or less. It is also nearly impossible to prevent the execution of an irrational order placed with a human representative of a discount brokerage firm since the order-taker is not the customer's own broker who would be more likely to know the customer's needs. Even if you have a full service broker who knows you and your needs, an irrational or inconsistent order creates a conflict between a customer's rights to control his or her own money and the broker's obligation to act in a customer's best interests. In most cases, brokers will execute a firm, unsolicited order (after efforts to talk the customer out of it fail), but to protect themselves, the broker may report the transaction to the firm's compliance officer and may even "fire" the customer to avoid future liability.

Of course, the easiest way to protect a needed stream of lifetime income is to convert at least some of the risky assets in the brokerage account to an immediate life annuity that cannot be discontinued. However, as previously discussed, the tiny proportion of the population

172

that actually buys an immediate annuity indicates that relatively few investors are willing to take this solution.

Safeguarding Online Brokerage Accounts

How can you obtain the benefits of inexpensive investment management while protecting yourself and your family from possible impaired investment decisions that you might make in the future? Here are a few suggestions:

If you are married, try to set up your brokerage account as a joint "and" account. Most joint brokerage accounts are "or" accounts which means that either party may make trades or access funds. An "and" account would require approval from both parties to make trades or withdraw funds. This puts one's partner in the position of being able to look over all transactions before they occur and intercede in those that don't look right. Unfortunately, I have found no investment companies that are willing to offer "and" accounts, perhaps because such an account would limit investment activity which generates commissions. Also, by offering an account that can protect aging clients from their own possible mistakes, brokers and financial advisors could lose a selling point for their investment management services.

Split the joint assets between two accounts, perhaps with separate brokerage companies, and have each party control one such account with account information such as passwords kept from the other. This will diversify the assets so that one irrational partner cannot jeopardize all the family assets.

Divide the password of an online brokerage account into two parts, with each party maintaining control of half. An easy way to do this (which has been used for hundreds of years) is to take a dollar bill and cut the serial number in half (you will have to do this twice because the serial number is repeated.) The serial number is entered as the password and then the cut-up dollar bill is distributed for safekeeping to both parties so that each knows only half the password. For further protection, the email name used to open the brokerage account should be the party who is least likely to trade in the account. In that way, if the primary trader claims to have lost the password to get a new one, it would come to his partner rather than himself.

Another possible solution would be to have all funds flow into and out of the brokerage account through a dual signature bank or money market account. This would prevent one party from draining funds from the brokerage account without the approval of the other party. Many banks will allow you to set up a dual signature checking account with two signature lines. You will often see such checks written by corporations or not-for-profit organizations. Some will specify a threshold level that requires dual signatures, such as $500 or $1,000. Checks written for amounts below that level might only require a single signature.

Unfortunately, while a few banks will still print checks that ostensibly require dual signatures, I have not yet found one that will *enforce* a dual signature requirement. In other words, if you try to cash a dual signature check at the teller line of your bank with only one signature present, an alert teller may note that you lacked a signature and refuse to cash it. However, if you used the check to pay for something or deposited the check in another account, it would be paid (processed) and you would not have legal recourse from the bank. This is just another example of a financial system that has not yet realized that its growing proportion of senior citizens needs protections that were commonplace in the past.

The Online, Unmanaged Portfolio

Probably the least expensive portfolio of investments that one could set up to manage itself and achieve the investor's objectives of safety and cash flow involves an online account consisting of low-cost Exchange Traded Funds (ETFs). Some of the largest ETFs are index funds which mirror the performance of the entire stock market and cost the investor less than one tenth of one percent per year in expenses. Since this is one fifteenth, or less, of the fees charged by most financial planners, brokers or other wealth managers who are given legal power to manage your investments, it has great appeal to those who are looking to maximize their returns or don't wish to entrust anyone else with their assets.

Three important characteristics of ETFs for those looking to set up a reasonably safe, diversified and inexpensive unmanaged account, are:
1.   The size of the ETF
2.   The broadness of the index that it tracks
3.   Its expense ratio or annual holding cost.

Size matters in ETFs, in part because large ETFs are widely traded and liquid which means that you will lose little to trading costs when you buy and sell. ETFs that follow a broad index tend to be well-diversified which means that trouble experienced by one underlying company will not bring down the price of the ETF by very much.

There are now thousands of ETFs to choose from, including those that are actively managed (which tend to have high expense ratios) and those that are highly speculative. Investors who seek to set up an unmanaged account may be interested in low expense ratio index funds or stocks and fixed income securities.

Listed in Table 2 as examples, are index ETFs which are large (more than $10 billion in assets) and low cost (one tenth of one percent or less in annual expenses). Three of these are S&P500 Index ETFs which track the most representative index of larger companies listed on the stock exchanges of the US. The S&P 500 index tends to pay annual dividends equal to about 2 percent of the value of the investment. One ETF tracks investment grade bonds in the US and is a useful way of creating income with an average yield of about 4 percent in 2013. Another tracks Real Estate Investment Trusts (REITs) which own all types of investment real estate in the US including office buildings, shopping centers, apartment houses and storage units among other things. REITs also generate income in the form of dividends, most recently a little over 3 percent, but also tend to increase with inflation.

Table 2
Examples of ETFs That Are Large and Low-Cost

Type	Symbol	Name	Assets	Expense Ratio
Stock	SPY	SPDR S&P 500 Index	140 bil.	.09%
Stock	IVV	iShares S&P 500 Index	43 bil.	.07%
Stock	VOO	Vanguard S&P 500	10 bil.	.05%
Bond	BND	Vanguard Barclays US Investment Grade Bond Index	18 bil.	.10%
REIT	VNQ	Vanguard MSCI US REIT Index	21 bil.	.10%

An easy way to create an unmanaged portfolio with an online broker is to first decide the annual income that you will need from that account and then set up the account to generate that amount of income. For example, if you need to draw a solid 4 percent of your investment to supplement your other income each year, you might choose to purchase an investment grade ETF bond fund which has a record of paying out that amount over several years. While investment grade bonds are not without some risk in the event of a very severe economic downturn (which could cause some investment grade companies to go out of business,) they are generally thought to be secure.

If you only need to draw 3 percent from your investment, a 50/50 split between bond and stock index ETFs would give you the regular income you needed and some growth potential over time. If you needed just 2 percent, an all-stock index ETF would get the job done.

It should be emphasized that the purpose of this section is *not* to give you investment advice, but rather to explain how you could easily set up an investment portfolio that doesn't really need management (from you or anyone else) to meet your objectives of safety, cash flow and growth at the lowest possible cost. By not having to manage your account, you are less likely to trade unnecessarily, or (worse) speculate or (even worse) access your needed capital to do irrational things for yourself or for others who may wish to manipulate you.

If trading stocks is something that you enjoy, you would be well advised to partition your capital into two accounts: an unmanaged account with the bulk of the investment funds on which you depend, and a much smaller "play" account that you will manage.

When my father was in his late 80s, he would tell me that he sold his Texaco and bought GE because of something he read in the *Wall Street Journal*. As an investments professor who realized that even the pros with their $20,000/year Bloomberg terminals couldn't routinely beat the market, I should have objected, but I didn't. My dad "played" with about 10 percent of his money, moving from one blue chip company to another, generating income for his broker, sure, but also having some fun.

My mother enjoyed going to Las Vegas and gambling her money in another way, and I could see little difference between the two of them. As long as they didn't touch *serious* capital, why shouldn't they have their fun. A segregated "unmanaged' account, which contained their serious capital would provide the protection that they needed. By using any of the methods suggested above to make access to the serious account difficult, they would have been even better protected.

Treasury Direct

If you're looking for regular income with no risk and no *cost*, nothing beats an account with the US Treasury. I refer to the Treasury Direct Account which you can open by email and which charges no commission or management fees for the bonds that you buy and hold through the account. Not only that, but your interest comes to your bank account twice a year and you can structure your account to also pay out its principal on a regular basis if you want the account to be self-liquidating over a number of years.

But wait, there's more! You can choose between regular Treasury bonds (or "notes" which have maturities of 1 to 10 years) and TIPS, the inflation-protected bonds discussed throughout this book. And finally, the Treasury makes it somewhat difficult to get at your principal (sell your bonds) so that you are well-protected from your future irrational self.

You can open a Treasury Direct Account by going to the government web site https://www.treasurydirect.gov/RS/UN-AccountCreate.do. You will be asked to supply your email address, bank account and bank routing number (from the bottom of your check), and then you will be asked to fill out some personal information, create a password and choose some security details. When approved by the Treasury, they will send you an email with your account number.

Logging on to your Treasury Direct Account is not difficult for those who still possess full cognitive powers. However, the combination of a long account number (10 characters) that they assign to you plus a complex password that *you must enter on a scrambled keyboard on the screen* pretty well guarantees that you won't be able to tamper with your portfolio in your dotage. This is good!

You can buy regular Treasury notes and bonds as well as TIPS at *auctions* which occur throughout the year. This is not as complex as it may seem. On the Treasury Direct web site you can see the forthcoming auctions which tell you the type of bond that is being offered, whether it is a TIPS or a regular bond, the date of the auction and the yield of the bonds if they end up being sold at (or close to) par (basically $1,000). Nearly all individuals enter what is called a non-competitive bid by indicating in an online form which bonds you would like to buy and how much you would like to invest in those bonds.

Suppose that the upcoming auction is offering 14 year Treasury bonds with a yield (at par) of 3 percent and you would like to buy 20 of them for $20,000. As a non-competitive bidder, you are guaranteed to get 20 of those bonds, but the actual price that you will pay for them may be more or less than the par value of $1,000 each depending on the demand of the non-competitive bidders, who are generally large financial institutions. In general, the price that you will actually pay will be slightly higher or lower than $1,000 per bond since the Treasury officials have a pretty good idea of demand before the bonds go to auction. If you pay a little over $1,000 per bond (called a "premium" price), your yield will be a tiny bit lower than the stated yield. Conversely, if you pay a little under $1,000 per bond (called a "discount" price), your yield will be slightly higher than the stated yield. In any event, after the auction the Treasury will withdraw the amount you have paid for the bonds ($20,000, more or less) and will put the bonds in your Treasury Direct account.

Twice a year, beginning 6 months after you bought the bonds, your bank account will be credited with the interest. If you have 20 bonds, this will come to 3 percent of $20,000 divided by 2 (for twice a year payments) which equals $300. At the maturity of your bond, 14 years in our example, your bank account will be credited with the par value of the bonds, $20,000, in addition to the last interest payment of $300.

If you wanted to get regular payments of more than the interest on your bonds, you could "ladder" the bonds by purchasing, at auction, bonds that matured when you wanted the payments. For example, if you had $150 thousand to invest and you wanted payments of $10,000 per year in addition to your interest, you could accumulate at auction $10,000 each of 1,2,3,4,5,6,7,8,9,and 10 year notes as well as 11, 12, 13, 14 and 15 year bonds. Since $10,000 of your investment will mature each year, you will receive regular payments of $10,000 plus interest each year in your bank account without having to do anything. The only drawback is that bonds and notes that mature soon tend to earn less in interest than longer maturity bonds (particularly now when the Fed has forced short maturity notes to nearly zero).

Managed Payout Accounts

There are even simpler, but somewhat more costly methods of getting regular income to cover your expenses so you won't be tempted to meddle with and possibly risk your safe investment portfolio. Vanguard's "Managed Payout Funds", for example, consist of a group of Vanguard mutual funds, purchased online, and chosen to provide regular monthly payments. There are three funds to choose from, each with a different payout percentage and degree of risk.

• **Managed Payout Growth Focus Fund** which has a relatively low monthly payout, higher risk and good growth potential.

• **Managed Payout Growth and Distribution Fund** which has moderate payout, risk and growth potential

• **Managed Payout Distribution Focus Fund** which has a high monthly payout, low risk and small growth potential.

If you go to Vanguard's web site, you will find a calculator that tells you how much you must invest in each of the funds to produce an estimated monthly income. For example, in May 2013, I asked it to compute the size of an investment needed to produce $2,000 in monthly income if invested in the most conservative Managed Payout Distribution Focus Fund and it said I needed to invest $362,558 to generate that amount of monthly income. The web site may be found at https://personal.vanguard.com/us/funds/vanguard/Managed PayoutList.

While the intent of the fund is to produce $2,000 per month indefinitely, it cannot guarantee this performance since it is invested in securities that vary with the market. In its disclaimer, it points out that "The fund's strategic objective is to try to maintain the dollar value of an investor's original investment and payment amounts over the long term. However, the inflation adjusted value of the fund shares and payment amount is expected to decrease over time. Additionally, if the fund's investment returns are low, the fund may distribute capital as part of its payout, which could lead to a decline in the dollar amount of monthly payment amounts and in the value of fund shares over time."

It is also important to note that the fund charges just a shade over a half percent per year in fees. This is about a third of what you are likely to be charged by a planner or broker who manages your account.

2.2 I Manage My Own Financial Assets but Take Investment Recommendations from a Broker

The previous section looked at the pros and cons of managing your investments yourself and showed how it could be done. While this method is least expensive, costing close to nothing per year for buy and hold investors (particularly for those who use TreasuryDirect which is free), it does require thought and understanding of the process up front. If a portfolio is structured to automatically achieve (most of) your retirement investment objectives, it does not have to be revisited and offers a degree of protection against the possibility that you will meddle with it if your cognitive ability declines.

If you don't have the ability to structure a low-cost, low-management portfolio yourself, you may seek out the services of a fee-only financial planner who is willing to do this for a one-time fee based on the hours spent. If you can find such an honest and capable planner in your area, this could be a wonderful solution. However, as covered earlier in the book, most such capable planners strongly prefer to manage your portfolio themselves, for an annual fee of about 1.5 percent of your assets. More on this in the next section.

Many investors choose to select their retirement investment portfolio with the help of full-service stockbrokers who charge a commission on sales that they make to you. The normal full commission charged by full-service brokers averages about 2 percent of the purchase or sales price of the securities, but those with larger portfolios can generally negotiate a rate of half that or less.

There are several advantages of using a full-service broker. They are required to know something about you and your investment needs and objectives under the "know your customer" rule and are also prohibited from making recommendations to you that are not "suitable" to your needs. Some brokers are both knowledgeable and ethical and are capable and willing to help you choose a buy-and-hold portfolio that meets your retirement income and safety objectives with little or no additional management. We have profiled one such broker, Jim, in this book. The question is whether they will be willing to do that for you.

Consequently, if you are fortunate enough to locate an ethical broker who is capable of suggesting a mix of low-fee index ETFs that will create a portfolio that needs little management (turnover) to achieve your retirement investment objectives, don't expect that broker to be enthusiastic about taking on the job. While first year commissions will be high as the portfolio is purchased, commissions in subsequent years will be negligible since little or no additional turnover will be needed.

Full-service brokerage firms can provide you with many services. Their brokers tend to be well-trained and knowledgeable, their account statements are generally accurate and well-organized and their support staff is often invaluable in answering questions and solving problems. Many will even protect you if they find a suspicious charge to your account or check that you may or may not have written. Finally, their compliance department is generally first rate in monitoring your broker's actions to insure that the broker is not suggesting or executing unsuitable trades or "churning" your account with a high turnover rate designed to generate commissions.

These important services are costly to your broker, however, since they can involve a lot of time of valuable professionals. The cost of supporting a client of a full-service broker can be several thousand dollars per year. If you, the client, are not generating that level of income, you are losing money for your broker. Therefore, in seeking a brokerage relationship which can provide you with many valuable services at a lower cost than a wealth manager who charges a flat fee for assets under management, you must evaluate your attractiveness to the broker.

Full-service brokerage firms have tended, in recent years, to limit their customer base to those who are profitable now or who have such large assets that they are likely to be profitable in the future. This has meant that they have encouraged clients with low balances (say, under a quarter of a million dollars) who are unwilling to have their assets managed for them and who do not generate much in the way of commissions, to do their business elsewhere. The bigger your balance, the more attractive you are to a brokerage firm and the more likely you are to be able to interest a broker with a great reputation for service and reliability to take on your account.

What Will My Broker Do for Me if I Get Stupid?

Commission clients of full service brokerage firms are supposed to be protected by "know your customer" and "suitability" rules. This means that your broker should have asked you questions regarding your investment objectives, the amount of risk that you are willing to accept and the income that you would like to generate, among other things. Your responses are generally coded on your customer account so that they can be brought up during discussions that you have with your broker. In addition, the brokerage firm's compliance department should be evaluating investment orders executed by your broker for their suitability, given your stated investment needs.

While suitability standards are enforced for orders generated by suggestions made by your broker, they are often not enforced very carefully for unsolicited orders. Nor is the law clear enough at this point to place much responsibility on the broker who carries out an order for an investment that he or she did not recommend. That is why such order slips and confirmations will say boldly "unsolicited" on them to place the onus on the customer rather than the brokerage firm if the investment fares badly.

The question of "suitability" is often interpreted with great latitude. You may have a portfolio consisting of highly-rated utility stocks that pay large dividends needed for your retirement. One day, having seen a manic analyst on television recommend a volatile high tech stock that pays no dividend but has "great growth potential," you put in an unsolicited order to sell your reliable utility holdings and put all your money in the speculative high tech stock. Your buy and sell orders will be stamped "unsolicited" and it is very likely that both will be executed, even though the

185

transaction is not well-suited to your needs. If, however, you tried to buy stock on margin or to buy options or futures or even penny stocks, it is likely that your order will be flagged as unsuitable by the computer or the broker. If you have not given your broker power of attorney to manage your portfolio, the broker generally has no fiduciary obligation to handle your unsolicited investments in your best interest.

Therefore, if you present your commissioned broker with a request to give you a test of cognitive capability whenever you call, you are unlikely to find your request honored. In most cases, your unsolicited orders will be executed without question, no matter how bizarre, as long as they are generally deemed to be "suitable" under very broad standards. In fact, since placing an order with a human broker is easier than it is online, where you have to remember or retrieve a password, it may offer fewer protections to us when we have diminished cognitive capacity.

2.3 My Financial Assets are Controlled by a Broker, Planner or Asset Manager

While it is possible to compensate those who give you financial advice through the payment of commissions on financial products that you buy or sell, it is becoming more commonplace to compensate them based upon the assets that they manage for you. A large proportion of retirement assets these days are controlled by a broker, planner or asset manager who has been given legal power to manage them on your behalf. The cost for this service is typically in the vicinity of 1.5 percent of assets under management which generally includes commission costs so you don't have to pay twice. It is sometimes possible to lower this fee by selecting a portfolio that doesn't need a lot of active management, such as a portfolio of bonds or mutual funds.

There are a lot of things that a good asset manager or financial planner can do for you. These include:

•   Setting up a portfolio that will generate the regular income that you need for the rest of your life without taking on much risk.

•   Making sure that you are protected against inflation as well as a severe market downturn.

•   Minimizing the tax liability that could be generated by trading your portfolio too much. Assets that you hold in taxable form (i.e., other than tax-sheltered retirement assets such as IRAs) should seldom be traded to keep from generating needless capital gains. Adjustments in assets should generally be made in your tax-sheltered accounts.

•   Adjusting your portfolio as your need for regular income changes. This may result (negatively) from a deterioration in health or (positively) from downsizing a home.

•   Adjusting your portfolio to changes in the tax code. If the tax rate on dividends increases relative to the tax rate on interest, it may be useful to hold fewer stocks and more bonds.

•   Monitoring your checks, money transfers and debit card use to guard against fraud.

•   Helping you in times of emergency or great change such as the loss of a spouse, serious illness or damage to your home.

•   Communicating your investment tax information accurately and in a timely fashion to your tax preparer.

A good asset manager should know your needs and investments very well, should be up to date on tax laws and useful investment products, should talk with you regularly and should be reachable at short notice. But what, if any, responsibility should your asset manager have to monitor your ability to conduct your financial affairs in a competent manner?

Frequent communication could enable the asset manager to determine whether you have suffered a sudden decline in cognitive ability. In your client agreement, you should spell out exactly what he or she should do if it appears as if you are no longer fully rational. This may necessitate a call to your spouse, to a trustee other than your spouse, to a child or to a health professional. As mentioned earlier, you could also specify a test of cognition as part of your client agreement. Many wealth managers will be willing to do this to keep your account.

Yet one of the advantages of having a wealth manager is that it minimizes your own responsibility for handling your investments. Since you are paying someone to perform the functions itemized above, you have greatly reduced your ability to damage your financial position as a result of diminished financial capability.

There are some things that an asset manager should not be expected to do. Foremost among these is the expectation that he or she will be able to outperform the market on a regular basis, particularly without taking on additional risk. Few, if any, investment professionals regularly outperform the market and if they could, why would they be spending their time managing your meager assets when they could be running multi-billion dollar mutual funds or hedge funds which would pay them millions (even billions) of dollars per year.

In fact, relatively few asset managers actually spend much time managing your assets. To set up a portfolio that best meets your needs, you will be asked to fill out a detailed questionnaire about your assets, income, expenses, needs, wants, objectives and attitudes toward risk. This is often analyzed by a computer and an investment profile will be generated for you. This investment profile will generally be used to structure your investment portfolio which may consist of large and small cap US stocks, foreign stocks, laddered US and foreign government and corporate bonds and some cash. Few wealth managers have the time or expertise to structure or keep track of all these moving pieces, so they tend to subcontract the management of your portfolio to outside money managers often called investment advisory firms. This is often done through "separately managed accounts" (SMAs) for each component of your portfolio (domestic stocks, foreign stocks, domestic bonds, foreign bonds, etc.). These separately managed accounts may also be called "separate accounts" or "private accounts."

Each component of your portfolio will be handled by specialists. A US government bond specialist will handle your Treasury bonds. A small cap specialist will handle your investment in the stocks of smaller companies, etc. Rather than manage *your* money specifically, the specialized money managers will manage the money of hundreds or thousands of individuals whose needs are similar to yours. For example, if your profile shows a great deal of risk aversion, your large cap stock investments may be placed into a "capital preservation" portfolio along with many other investors with similar needs. If the money manager fears an economic downturn, he or she may sell some of the stocks and hold cash until the fear passes, or "rotate" into "defensive" stocks that tend to do better than others during economic downturns. Grocery stores, for example, tend to do better than airlines during a recession since people have to eat but don't have to fly.

While "active management" of stocks (as opposed to buying and holding a broad stock index) has not been shown to outperform passive management (after expenses)

189

over time, this does not mean that a cautious and skilled capital preservation manager cannot protect you from the worst effects of a significant downturn. And since many retired individuals favor preservation of their capital over growth, this service may be very worthwhile to you.

Wealth managers, including brokers and planners, typically pay about half of one percent (50 basis points) of your assets to the outside money managers for handling the funds placed in separate managed accounts. The fee charged to you depends both on the amount of money that you have under management and how your portfolio divides between stocks and bonds. Management fees for a "small" stock portfolio of under $1 million can be as high as 3 percent in a large firm such as Merrill-Lynch.

Even if you are charged less, say, 1 ½ percent of your assets for money management of a reasonably-sized portfolio, subtracting the ½ percent fee charged to your money manager by the outside asset manager leaves your manager about 1 percent to pay for the accounting and record keeping that they do for your account as well as the customer support that they and their staffs give to you. Some large brokerage firms will charge less to manage your money if you allow them to purchase a variety of special purpose mutual funds rather than placing your assets in separately managed accounts. Merrill Lynch, for example, offers a mutual fund advisor program in which accounts with assets of more than $1 million are charged a fee of ½ of 1 percent in addition to the wholesale ("institutional share class") rates of ½ to 4/5 of a percent that it pays the mutual funds. The total fee for this service turns out to be about two-thirds of that charged for separately managed accounts of the same asset size.

If you have a good wealth manager who understands and meets your needs and who insures that your portfolio is competently managed to your needs by the experts of well-known outside money managers, you may well be getting your money's worth. This is particularly true if your wealth manager formally agrees to monitor your conversations for signs of cognitive impairment, with or without the aid of a script, and make appropriate referrals as per your instructions to protect your assets and possibly even yourself. Frequent contact with your wealth manager can enable him or her to talk with you about any changing financial needs you might have as well as to better detect changes in your ability to understand your finances.

Conclusion

This chapter has provided some practical approaches to two of the major problems addressed by this book. The first problem is how we can best structure our finances so that they can provide sufficient income for the rest of our lives. The second related problem is how we can best protect this income against possible irrational decisions that we may make as we get older.

Relatively few of us will have guaranteed inflation-proof lifetime income sufficient to maintain or even enhance our current lifestyles. Therefore, most of us will be forced to consider at least some tweaks to our finances. If we worry about the possibility of outliving our regular sources of income, we should at least consider supplementing that income with an immediate annuity. This chapter tells us how to start that process. If much of our income is subject to erosion by inflation, we explain how an immediate annuity which adjusts to the cost of living or an investment in Treasury Inflation Protected Securities (TIPS) can give us protection. If we are short of both regular, inflation-protected income *and* the financial assets needed to generate more lifetime income, we need to make some hard choices about lifestyle which often begins by downsizing our housing or using a reverse mortgage to convert home equity to a lifetime stream of income.

An advantage of Social Security retirement payments, many regular pension plans and most immediate annuities is that we can't terminate them in an irrational moment and jeopardize our futures. This is not true about financial assets that we own directly and hold in the form of bank deposits, stocks bonds or other securities. In this chapter we have considered the three most common means of managing those financial assets. We can manage some or all of them completely by ourselves by holding them in an online brokerage account (or discount broker). This is the least expensive method of holding assets and, if done right, may provide necessary additional income by eliminating nearly all of the fees charged by brokers or wealth managers. The downside of this thrifty method is that we are given little protection from irrational actions that we may take in the future that could threaten our lifetime income. Possible solutions are given to this problem in the chapter including the structuring of a low-maintenance portfolio which produces regular income and which has the added benefit of minimizing trading. Other possible solutions focus on mechanical safeguards to prevent our "raiding" our accounts in the future.

A second possible method of holding wealth is with the help of a full-service broker who charges trading commissions. If the account is not traded regularly, this method is more expensive than using an online or discount broker but less expensive than having the funds completely managed by an investment advisor. In comparison to an online or discount broker who makes no suggestions for investments, trading orders suggested by a full-service broker may provide some protection to the customer because they must be legally "suitable" to the customer's needs. If a broker is also a registered investment advisor, as many are these days, a higher level of "fiduciary" care for the needs of the customers may come into play. However, unsolicited orders, made by the customer without the broker's recommendation, may be executed even if they are not in the customer's best interests. Some brokers may be willing to agree, in writing, to decline seemingly irrational orders and carry out the customer's instructions to notify a close relative or trustee, but chances are that many will not because they are unwilling to accept the liability that is involved.

The highest level of protection against possible future irrationality is provided by wealth managers who are given the power to manage your assets. However, this is the most expensive type of asset management ranging from one to 3 or more percent of your assets per year. It also exposes you to the possible loss of your assets through risky or unscrupulous behavior on the part of the asset manager.

A good wealth manager, who is honest, knowledgeable and caring, can well be worth the added management cost. Most will set up a portfolio that meets your needs for safety, growth and regular income. Since he or she has legal authority to manage your assets, you are given a fair amount of protection against your own poorly-considered financial decisions.

What to Do When I Get Stupid

NOTES

[1] Agarwal et. al. 2010 p2

[2] Salthouse, Timothy A. "Effects of Aging on Reasoning." In *The Cambridge Handbook of Thinking and Reasoning.* Cambridge, England: Cambridge University Press. Salthouse, Timothy A. (forthcoming). "Executive Functioning." In *Cognitive Aging: A Primer*, ed., edited by D. C. Park and N. Schwarz. London, UK: Psychology Press

[3] Lindenberger, Ulman, and Paul B. Baltes, 1994, Sensory functioning and intelligence in old age: A strong connection, Psychology and Aging 9, 339–355. Bates, Paul B., and Ulman Lindenberger, 1997, Emergence of a powerful connection between sensory and cognitive functions across the adult life span: A new window to the study of cognitive aging?, Psychology and Aging 12, 12–21

[4] Lindenberger & Bates 1997

[5] Masunaga, Hiromi, and John Horn, 2001, Expertise and age-related changes in components of intelligence, Psychology and Aging 16, 293–311

[6] Ferri at al 2005 [Cleusa P Ferri PhD, Prof Martin Prince MD, Prof Carol Brayne PhD, Prof Henry Brodaty MD, Prof Laura Fratiglioni PhD, Prof Mary Ganguli MD, Kathleen Hall PhD, Kazuo Hasegawa MD, Prof Hugh Hendrie DSc, Prof Yueqin Huang PhD, Prof Anthony Jorm DSc, Colin Mathers PhD, Paulo R Menezes PhD, Elizabeth Rimmer MA, Marcia Scazufca Global prevalence of dementia: a Delphi consensus study *Lancet* 366(0503): 2112-17 Dec. 2005

[7] Plassman, Brenda L., Kenneth M. Langa, Gwenith G. Fisher, Steven G. Heeringa, David R. Weir, Mary Beth Ofstedal, James R. Burke, Michael D. Hurd, Guy G. Potter, Willard L. Rodgers, David C. Steffens, Robert J. Willis, and Robert B. Wallace. !'""%., "Prevalence of Dementia in the United States: The Aging, Demographics and Memory Study. *Neuroepidemiology* 29:125-132

[8] Agarwal et al 2010

[9] Sumit Agarwal, John C Driscoll, Xavier Gabaix and David Laibson "The Age of Reason: Financial Decisions over the Life-Cycle with Implications for Regulation." October 19, 2009 Prepared for the *Broookings Papers on Economic Activity, p 9-11*

[10] ibid

[11] George M. Korniotis and Alok Kumar "Do Older Investors Make Better Investment Decisions?" *Review of Economics and Statistics,* 93 (1), 244-265, 2011

[12] Michael S. Finke, John Howe, and Sandra J. Huston "Old Age and the Decline in Financial Literacy," Texas Tech University, unpublished manuscript 2012

[13] Ibid p 15

[14] Holland and Rabbitt, 1992

[15] Finke, et. al, op cit p16

[16] Anderson 2007 (cited in AARP)

[17] **AARP Foundation National Fraud Victim Study** March 2011

[18] Lona Choi-Allum "Protecting Older Investors: 2009 Free Lunch Seminar Report," AARP *Surveys and Statistics, November 2009.*

[19] Helaine Olen *Pound Foolish,"* New York: Penguin Books, 2012, p122

[20] **Elder Investment Fraud and Financial Exploitation: A Survey Conducted for the Investor Protection Trust** June 15, 2010

[21] An excellent book that focuses on this point is *Risk Less and Prosper: Your Guide to Safer Investing,"* by Zvi Bodie and Rachelle Taqqu,* Hoboken, NJ: John Wiley & Sons, 2012

[22] Tara Siegel Bernard "Budget Negotiating Chip Has Big Downside for Old and Poor," *New York Times* April 19, 2013

[23] See Bodie, Zvi, "Inflation Protection for Pension Plans," Compensation & Benefits Management Vol. 6, Issue 2,Winter1990, pp105-110

[24] If the pension is not fully funded, there may be some risk attached to it. Pensions of companies that go bankrupt are generally taken over by the federal Pension Benefit Guarantee

Corporation (PBGC) although the greatest pension that may be paid in 2012 was $54,000 per year and cost of living adjustments (COLAs) are not paid by the PBGC. In 2009, 44 million Americans were covered by 29 thousand defined benefit pension plans. Defined benefit pensions of states, cities and counties that go bankrupt are not protected by the PBGC and these pensions may be reduced.

[25] If you own Treasury bonds that you bought several years ago at rates higher than you are paying on your mortgage, you may disagree with this statement. However, the fall in the rates of Treasury bonds has increased the value of those bonds to the point where your return on the bonds is now below your mortgage rate.

[26] Adjusted for inflation

[27] This assumes that the $150,000 will grow to $165,000 between now and when the funds must be paid out

[28] "Should You Purchase Long-Term-Care Insurance?" *Wall Street Journal,* May 14, 2012

[29] This assumes that current proposals by some politicians to greatly reduce Medicaid will not come to fruition.

[30] American Association for Long Term Care Insurance http://www.aaltci.org/long-term-care-insurance/learning-center/ways-to-save.php

[31] Some continuing care retirement communities may offer variants on "life care" which covers the resident from independent living to skilled nursing care for the same monthly price. So-called "modified" contracts are often less expensive but cover only some health-care services; fees increase when a resident's needs exceed those services. Residents on fee-for-service contracts must pay for all health-related services. Finally, rental agreements, generally require no entrance fee, but residents must pay for all the services they receive.

[32] US General Accountability Office *Continuing Care Retirement Communities Can Provide Benefits, but Not Without Some Risk* Report to the Chairman, Special Committee on Aging, U.S. Senate, June 2010

[33] These deposits may or may not be refundable, depending upon the contract

[34] "Continuing-Care Retirement Communities: Weighing the Risks," *Wall Street Journal* August 7,2010

[35] Without an influx of relatively healthy, younger residents, the average age of the community increases as does the cost of health care. This lack of subsidization of the old by the young puts added financial strain on the CCRCs.

[36] "Continuing-Care Retirement Communities: Weighing the Risks," *Wall Street Journal* August 7,2010

[37] A good description of the annuity puzzle is given by Pamela Perun in an Aspen Institute White Paper entitled *Retirement Savings: Confronting the Challenge of Longevity,"* 2010

[38] Franco Modigliani, Nobel Prize acceptance speech, December 9, 1985.

[39] Jeffrey R. Brown "Understanding the Role of Annuities in Retirement Planning," in Annamaria Lusardi (editor) *Overcoming the Saving Slump: How to Increase the Effectiveness of Financial Education and Saving Programs,* University of Chicago Press, 2008, pp182-83

[40] Economists call this "longevity risk"

[41] In the real world, this would be reduced by a little to pay for the operations and profit of the insurance company

[42] Typically called a Guaranteed Minimum Income Benefit (GMIB) which adds to the cost of the annuity

[43] Based on the 2007 Social Security Periodic Life Table http://www.ssa.gov/oact/STATS/table4c6.html

[44] $88,929 to be specific

[45] Annuities purchased by corporations are generally unisex

[46] This can be calculated using a financial calculator or Excel using 13.73 for N, $1 million for Present Value, $78,312 for Payment, solve for I/Y. As we will see later in this chapter, those who buy annuities tend to live longer than others their age so the expected payout will be for more than 13.73 years which makes the actual interest rate higher than 1 percent.

[47] Claude Penland "Life Insurance Salary Survey," http://www.claudepenland.com/2010/09/10/life-insurance-

salary-survey-%e2%80%93-10-companies-c-level-underlying-data-available/

[48] New TIPS are sold at auction and sometimes buyers are willing to pay more than their face value of $1,000 per bond, driving the real rate of return negative

[49] The clever reader will note that your *lifetime* income is not increased by 8% since every year you wait to begin taking your Social Security payments; you are a year older and closer to death. However, in today's interest rate environment, getting an additional 8% *fully adjusted for inflation* is a terrific deal, well worth taking for those who are healthy

[50] Brown, op cit, p184

[51] ibid

[52] For age 60 it is 24.2, for age 65 it is 20.0, for age 75 it is 12.5. IRS Publication 939 General Rules for Pensions and Annuities, Table V

[53] On September 21, 2012, 5 year TIPS paid -1.5%, 7 year paid -1.17%, 10 year paid -0.71%, 20 year paid 0.05% and 30 year paid 0.46%

[54] http://www.money-zine.com/Financial-Planning/Retirement/Inflation-Protected-Annuities/

[55] This is calculated by using life expectancy as N, $100,000 as the Present Value (PV) and the annual payment of $7,149/year as the Payment (PMT) and solving for the internal rate of return for the non-inflation-protected annuity. If N = 13, the IRR is equal to -1.03%. We compare this to the IRR for the inflation-protected annuity which pays 5,241/year and find it to be -5.08%. Since (1+ the real rate of return) multiplied by (1+expected inflation) = (1 + the nominal rate of return) the expected rate of inflation comes out to be 4.09%. If this process is done again for a 15 year life expectancy, the expected rate of inflation is 3.72%.

[56] However, the market value of your TIPS can decline before maturity if real rates of return suddenly increase. This is unlikely to have a big effect on the value of your TIPS since most changes in bond values are due to inflation, which is hedged by TIPS.

57 National Conference of Insurance Guarantee Funds (NCIGF)

[58] USAA was too small to be listed in this table

[59] Consumer Financial Protection Bureau *Ask CFPB **Mortgages***
"What happens if I have to move out of my home into a nursing home or assisted living and I have a reverse mortgage?" Updated Sept. 16, 2012

[60] Divide $650,000 by .667

[61] $650,000 divided by .544.

[62] The Mortgage Professor "HECMs and Fixed-Payment Annuities" December 21, 2009, Reviewed June 2, 2012. http://www.mtgprofessor.com/a%20-%20reverse%20mortgages/HECMs%20and%20Fixed%20Payment%20Annuities.html

[63] Although this flexibility does enable him to be swindled more easily than if he had purchased a single payment immediate annuity

[64] Hung, Angela A., Clancy Noreen, Jeff Dominitz, Eric Talley, Claude Berrebi, and Farrukh Suvankulov. 2008. Investor and Industry Perspectives on Investment Advisers and Broker-Dealers..Technical Report, Rand Institute for Civil Justice.

[65] Hackethal, Andreas and Roman Inderst. 2012. .How to Make the Market for Financial Advice Work..Paper prepared for the 2012 Pension Research Council Conference. Van Rooij, Marten, Rob Alessie, and Annamaria Lusardi. 2007. .Financial Literacy and Stock Market Participation..Unpublished.

[66] SEC "Investment Advisers: What You Need to Know Before Choosing One," online http://www.sec.gov/investor/pubs/invadvisers.htm

[67] *Financial Advisers, Police Yourselves*, by Spencer Bachus Wall Street Journal, August 6, 2012

[68] Jim may get a small amount of money each year from the mutual fund companies used by his clients. Called 12b-1 fees, after the name of the rule that authorized them, they are charged to mutual fund investors and are used to pay for marketing and distributions costs. These fees typically amount to less than 25 basis points or a quarter of a percent of the amount invested.

[69] SEC: Protect Your Money: Check Out Brokers and Investment Advisers. http://www.sec.gov/investor/brokers.htm

[70] Susan Antilla, "A Rise in Requests From Brokers to Wipe the Slate Clean," *New York Times* June 10, 2013

[71] Liz Skinner "Ex-NAPFA chairman diverted nearly $50M from clients: DOJ" *Investment News* May 17, 2012

[72] 1.5% of a million dollars under management generates a fee of $15,000 per year. If the account is sold for two times the annual fees, the price would be $30,000.

[73] The present value of $15,000 per year for 14 years at 3% is $169,441, still a decent amount

[74] Survey by FA Insight of Tacoma, Wash. Cited in Maxey, Daisy "How to Pay Your Financial Advisor," *Wall Street Journal,* December 12, 2011

[75] Some variable annuity plans will give you a guaranteed annual income but it will be a fraction of the guaranteed income of a single payment immediate fixed annuity

[76] Mary Williams Walsh and Danny Hakim "Public Pensions Faulted for Bets on Rosy Returns," *New York Times* May 27, 2012

[77] ibid

[78] Wade D. "Can We Predict the Sustainable Withdrawal Rate for New Retirees?" *Journal of Financial Planning* August 2011

[79] Mutual fund companies generally offer financial planners a "deal" by charging them only about 50 basis points to buy the fund from them "wholesale," allowing them to charge their clients 150 basis points or more for the fund and any advice they may give.

[80] Folstein MF, Folstein SE, McHugh PR (1975). ""Mini-mental state". A practical method for grading the cognitive state of patients for the clinician". *Journal of Psychiatric Research* **12** (3): 189–98

[81] https://www.marketpsych.com/resources/files/MEMRI_script_MarketPsych_2012-03-26.pdf

[82] The present value of $1,500 per year at 2% is $18,572

[83] 1.02 raised to the power of 30 minus 1

[84] However, there are two problems with buying TIPS to cover deficiencies in COLAs. First, unlike a defined benefit pension which pays you for life, the longest TIPS will only pay for 30 years which may be short for people who live into their late 90s (and long for those who die earlier). Second, even though TIPS adjust their value and their payments with increases in the cost of living, the amount of TIPS you must buy to cover annual fixed pension payments will vary with the average rate of inflation expected over the next 30 years.

[85] Interest on TIPS is actually paid twice a year and each interest payment is based on the consumer price index. Therefore, the actual interest earned depends on how much of the increase in the consumer price index has occurred in each 6-month period. The examples given here have been simplified to aid in understanding.

[86] Determined by subtracting the rate on 30 year TIPS from the rate on regular 30 year Treasury bonds.

[87] Based on using up the entire TIPS investment in 30 years. This assumes that TIPS will continue to pay an inflation-adjusted ("real") rate of return of about 2%.

[88] Inflationdata.com

[89] Shane Flait "Inflation Will Eat Up More Than Half Your Income after 25 Years of Retirement – Unless You Invest Right," http://www.sovereignu.com/articlecategories/ManagingRetirementIncome/wSYA0904302retinc-InflationseffectoverRetirementONEgraph.doc.htm

[90] $10,000/$5,241 times $100,000

[91] $10,000/$7,149 times $100,000

[92] $50,924, the added cost of inflation adjustment for a $10,000 annuity payment for a 70 year-old man multiplied by 3

[93] Jay Adkisson "Trust Protectors – What They Are and Why Probably Every Trust Should Have One." *Forbes* August 25, 2012 http://www.forbes.com/sites/jayadkisson/2012/08/25/trust-protectors-what-they-are-and-why-probably-every-trust-should-have-one/

INDEX